How Are Things?

Roger-Pol Droit is a research fellow at the CNRS in Paris, and author of the bestselling *101 Experiments in the Philosophy of Everyday Life* (Faber, 2002).

Translator Theo Cuffe was educated in Dublin and at the Sorbonne. He has also translated Saint-Exupéry's *The Little Princess* and Voltaire's *Micromégas and Other Short Fictions* and *Candide* for Penguin.

ROGER-POL DROIT

How Are Things?

A Philosophical Experiment

translated by Theo Cuffe

faber and faber

First published by Éditions Odile Jacob, Paris
as *Dernières nouvelles des choses* in 2003

First published in this translation in 2005
by Faber and Faber Limited
3 Queen Square London WC1N 3AU

Published in the United States by Faber and Faber Inc.
an affiliate of Farrar, Straus and Giroux LLC, New York

Typeset by Faber and Faber Limited
Printed in England by Mackays of Chatham plc,
Chatham, Kent

A CIP record for this book
is available from the British Library

ISBN 978-0-571-22373-2
ISBN 0-571-22373-7

10 9 8 7 6 5 4 3 2 1

for 'l'Oiseau', in the first place

He promised to write a fine work of philosophy for them, in suitably tiny script, in which they would discover the nature of things.

Voltaire, *Micromégas*, Chapter 7

Contents

TRIAL AND ERROR

PANIC

Instructions For Use

Take *none* of the assertions in this book seriously?
An exaggeration.

Take *all of them* seriously? More exaggeration.

Accept that the following assertions *might* be
accurate, and draw your own conclusions.

Conclusions will vary, depending on the person.

Well, How Are They?

He comes towards me, his hand held out. He says, 'Well, so how are things?' I reply automatically, 'Oh, not so bad, things are fine . . . And you?' 'Oh, not so bad,' he shrugs. Friends are waving to him, he must join them. I know him only by sight. I run into him occasionally, in the apartments of friends, at parties like this one, this evening. I am not really sure who he is.

'How are things?' What was he trying to say? The words, a few moments later, strike me as bizarre. I assume he was asking after my news. However, he did not say, 'How are you?' He did not say, 'How is it going?' He did not say, 'How is business?' He did not say, 'What are you up to these days?' He did not say, 'How is the family?' What he said was (I am sure of this, I can still hear the words), 'How are things?'

What things? How are *what* things? *All* things? Things *in general*? *Certain* things only? My things?

Which ones? Meaning what? I would do best to let the matter drop. He only meant to say hello, after all. No need to tie yourself in knots about it. Let's change the record.

No. Can't be done. The phrase keeps coming back – 'How are things?' over and over. I drink another glass of red wine, talk to a few more people. I embrace a girlfriend I haven't seen for a long time. I try to put the phrase behind me. In vain. The question sticks, burr-like. Try as I may to shake it off, it hangs around. It makes itself comfortable. It's still there, boring its slow way into my cranium. I resist as well as I may, try to fill my head with other phrases. But this one spreads, like a flare, like a fissure, steadily propagating, glowing in the dark.

'How are things?' Things – yes, of course, what else is there? But how are they? I do not know how they are, alas. Besides, do they have lives of their own? What kind of lives? And when things are going well, what sort of well? Enough! Things are neither well nor ill. And they don't go anywhere. No more to be said. Nothing to see, so move along there! Things are there, in their places, and that's that. Or alternatively they are not in their place, and that's that. They are neither well nor unwell. They have neither rise nor fall, neither life nor death, neither honour nor shame. They are mere whatsits, thingummies, mere . . . things, exactly so. The whole question is ludicrous.

Nevertheless. Time passes, and the question refuses to go away. It ramifies, it breeds. I have the impression, at moments, of glimpsing an impenetrable fathomlesssness to things, a *terra incognita* of inner silence. You ask me how things are doing, and I am struck dumb. I do not know how they are doing. This is normal. Are we ordinarily preoccupied by such questions? Do we ever try to find out how things are doing? Are we right or wrong not to concern ourselves? Should we not make an effort? But this is ridiculous. Yet the question abides. There I stand, at the party, unable any longer to hear what people are saying to me, unable to speak. This idiotic mantra refuses to stop revolving inside my head. No hope of thinking about other – things. I decide to take a walk through the village, perhaps even into the surrounding countryside.

The air is mild enough, the streets deserted, the night already well advanced. As I walk along the river, the questions crowd in upon me. They loom up from all sides, from the ground, from the trees, from the water, from the very stones underfoot.

They fall from the sky. The air itself thickens with queries undreamed of mere moments ago. Is the air a thing? Does a thing have to be solid? Does it exist in time? How long must it exist for in order to qualify as a thing? Would you describe a shirt as a thing? What about a drop of water? A soap bubble? A fly speck? Is there a single and unique overall thing, immense, infinite and absolute, within which we exist, encountering moment by moment the infinity of its disparate aspects and appearances? Or, on the contrary, is there a multiplicity of dissimilar substances and forms without end, without comparison, without connection, ever new and inexhaustibly distinct each from the other?

The further I walk, the more assailed I am by a horde of enigmas. I watch as a crowd of nameless realities arise, entities run wild, phenomena no longer defined or only partially covered by their names, piecemeal, like slack skin, dried up and cracked all over. Whatever we mean by the term 'thing' has become suddenly opaque, incomprehensible and multicoloured. The great mystery of things considered in their totality, this cacophony of competing presences, abruptly reveals itself to be nameless. Voiceless. Or is it I who have no ears? No head? No means of understanding them? I feel as if I have been deprived of my faculties, from one moment to the next, in a world hissing with strange chatter, incomprehensible gesturings and provocations. The world has become at once garrulous and mute.

Everything remains recognisable, but at an unaccustomed remove. The names remain. This is my shirt, this is my watch, over there is a boat, up above is the moon. But they no longer tell me anything. Is my shirt a thing in the same sense as my watch? Or as the moon? And what about the boat? Again the question arises: are there, lurking behind that one word, innumerable distinct universes? Do we talk of 'things' in order to mask a proliferation and plurality without end? Is everything held in one big bag marked 'things', the world's immense lumber room? Containing galaxies and paperclips, soaps and railroad shares, black holes, red giants and socks, doorknobs, jet planes, photocopying machines and horse-drawn ploughs? Among other things; and to name but a few.

One must add 'among-other-things-and-to-name-but-a-few' *ad infinitum*. For in the smallest nook or cranny there are jumbled together things whose nature and provenance are utterly different. I am thinking of my study, which is not especially crammed with Egyptian statuettes or mementoes from the four corners of the earth. Nevertheless, within a few feet of each other there cohabit a pebble picked up in Savatthi, near Benares, where the Buddha is said to have preached for the first time; lamps brought back from Sweden; a computer manufactured in Japan; a wooden Buddha carved by a Thai peasant, which I am very attached to because it is cracked; a piece of Parisian paving and the stud from a pedestrian crossing, both relics of May '68; a brass tap from the 1920s; and a minuscule Bulgarian icon. Among other things, and to name but a few – for I am listing these from memory. Things that come from a dozen different places, each speaking after its fashion of a way of life and a certain kind of human universe. These universes are all disjunct.

I sit down on a bench at the edge of the village, trying to put some order into the hordes of countless and incompatible things jostling inside my head. Hard things and soft things. Liquid and solid things. Things that come close to my body, in contact with my skin, whether continuously (clothes, underclothes) or momentarily (soaps, towels, handkerchiefs); things distant from my physical self. Things to touch and things for looking at, or looking through. Things for setting in motion and things that are motionless. Classification by size, by weight, by colour, by origin, by material. Simple things and compound things, things natural and artificial, handmade and mass produced, long-lasting or short-lived, bright or dark, things with and without buttons, one-of-a-kind or otherwise . . . No system of classification holds good. No sooner constructed than it falls to pieces. Everything gets very quickly muddled and the system is undone. Are there no families among things? Merely one thing next to another, lying where they fall, in mute cacophony? Everywhere I look there are things, more and more of them, without interruption, as far as the eye can see. A procession without end. An inconceivable proliferation. Things more numerous than the sands of touch, of sight, of understanding, even if I lived a multitude of lives.

How can one know the number of things in the world? Is a galaxy a thing? A star? A molecule? A quark? In an attempt to keep abreast of the tide, I have decided to exclude heavenly bodies from consideration; to disqualify particles, elements, atoms. Let us keep things simple. Let us take 'things' as referring to those objects made by man. Leaving stones, mosses, natural elements and empty shells all to one side . . . Everything except human things. Created on purpose by human agency.

How many are there? How many things of this kind are there on earth? Approximately, of course – a universal census of things is not, after all, on anyone's agenda. But it's none the less a fine idea. We would learn, for instance – in due course, when the census had been carried out – how many drinking straws there are in Alaska, or shoes in Mauritania, or computers in Patagonia, or the average number of sheets of paper per capita in the southern hemisphere. And all sorts of other indispensable items of knowledge, pleasant to mull over together on long, statistical evenings. But we have yet to reach that stage. All I need for the present is a rough estimate. So, how many things are there on earth? Name a figure, just for fun . . .

It would be absurd, after all, to claim to discover how things are going, without knowing – however approximately – how many of them there are out there. So let's make a calculation. Let's say there are at least six billion of us. And let's assume that half of us – the rich – own on average a thousand things each, counting paperclips, doorknobs and all those bits of string that might come in useful one day. And let's assume that the poor own a hundred things each. Which evens out at five hundred and fifty things per head, which sounds reasonable enough. Multiplied by six billion, this makes three thousand three hundred billion things on earth. At a rough guess. Who on earth would claim to know how it's going for three trillion three hundred billion of anything whatsoever?

You are going to say that mere or sheer numbers are quite irrelevant? That philosophers should occupy themselves solely with essences and concepts? That the quantity of actual things is of no importance. Of zero interest. That only the idea of the thing counts, our thinking the thing, our analysis of the thing, our metaphysics of the thing. Whether there exists only one thing, or several dozen things, or hundreds of billions – no difference! Or at least that is the line taken by the hard-liners. The true philosophers.

Or the false, the out-and-out false? Is anyone really persuaded that our encounter with external realities teaches us nothing? That their quantity is indifferent, their diversity without significance? That their variety, categories, genealogies and metamorphoses are as nothing – just so many irrelevant culs-de-sac? On the contrary. Things have no residence other than in their absolute singularity. Matter in this particular place, under this particular form. Displaying this colour and no other. This texture and no other. This degree of wear and tear and no other. Each thing is itself and no other.

Do we have to examine them one by one? Plant ourselves in front of each thing as before an individual, alone of all its kind? No longer talk of lamps or shoes, but bestow on each its proper name, as bearing witness to its unique existence? Even at the risk of no longer being able to speak or think, since these are activities which always and inevitably presuppose that we neglect differences for the sake of resemblances? Must we, to approach the diversity-without-end of things, sink into mute contemplation of this particular window shutter, this pebble in my hand, this plank of the bench on which I sit?

Do I really have no choice between describing things without ever touching them, or else contemplating each one in an aphasic silence? On the one hand, things are apprehended by thought, but always botched as far as their concrete singularity goes. On the other hand, things are grasped in their concrete reality, in their self-presence, but inevitably lost sight of where their totality is concerned. At one extreme, to know only the Idea, as intended to encompass all realities. At the other extreme, to apprehend each individual reality, one after the other, at the risk of never being able to combine them into any whole. I sit for a long time on my bench, watching the moon reflected in the river and bits of paper drifting past.

There must be a way out. A way of avoiding this blockage by extremes. Of moving forwards diagonally, through the middle. Of no longer being caught in the traps of philosophy. Of leaving behind this realm of either/or. Of not falling into the clutches of the one party while fleeing the other. Of walking straight but by indirections, if possible. Of noting things, fixing one's gaze on them, doggedly scrutinising. But reserving the right to remove oneself now and then, to see them from a distance, to make comparisons. To remain suspended, magnetised by this in-betweenness. Putting our best foot forward despite the impossibility of doing so. Yes, that's the idea.

To begin with, tell yourself that things are in effect folded propositions. Or the folds of ancient and vanished phrases. Or the solid residues of extinct words. I don't exactly know which path to take, but yes, in this general direction. I dream of recovering the ideas sealed inside some of the things woven into our everyday lives hour by hour, gesture by gesture.

By the end of this evening, I have decided to try an experiment. I will attempt to draw nearer to things, to spy on them. To set foot on the *terra incognita* where they live. To play the explorer. I have no idea how I will set about it. In any case, I shall note down my observations steadily, create a ship's log of my voyage. I expect the experiment to take some time. Let's say a year.

By the end, I may have some idea as to the meaning of the question, 'How are things?'

ASTONISHMENT

Heaven does not dispose things according to our wishes.
Corneille, *Pompey*, V, ii

Bowl

late evening, in the city,
beginning of autumn

I no longer even know what time it is. It got dark an age ago, after an interminable day. Far too many words. Why do we talk so much? And now it's starting to get chilly. The harbinger of autumn evenings. In the country, the night must be quite black now; you would have to pick your way without seeing the path ahead. I have a sudden urge for a *soupe à l'oignon*, with grated cheese on top, piping hot. A relic from the past. Once a peasant dish, now a curiosity for tourists. Happily, I still know where to go.

Set before me is a large bowl, steaming, still bubbling. Fragrant, crusted around the edges. Dark brown in some areas, almost black, tending to pale yellow in others. But what arrives is not a soup. More than the fumes, the steam, the waft of oven, what is set before me is a bowl. Solid, heavy, as if from the depths of time. From childhood and beyond. Prehistoric. A concave thing, protecting the liquid, preventing it from escaping. The shape of reassurance, instantly companionable and trust-worthy.

I almost forget what I am doing here, in the present. Here is one of the earliest, most primitive objects. This thing remembers the emergence of mankind. The larger primates had clubs, stones, rough likenesses of weapons and tools. But no bowls. Only with mankind do platters make an appearance: gourds, basins, bowls.

The bowl inaugurates the function of receptacle. It is a figure of reassurance. Amid the universal flux, the receptacle intervenes and stanches the endless flow. It preserves against dispersal. It prevents spillage. It suspends pouring. Liquid, which is fanatically committed to leakage and loss, is stayed. More effectively than by cupping one's hands. And indefinitely. Effortlessly.

The bowl permits some control over natural entropy. It intervenes in what is endlessly passing. It interposes itself in the universal stream, where otherwise, as Heraclitus said, 'everything flows'. It offers a controlled intervention, for it is *reversible*. This is the essential point. If the bowl imitates, so to speak, the rocky hollow or fissure, the most tri-fling of nature's cavities, it is not content with merely copying nature. It is not (after all) fixed in place. It can be turned upside down and emptied. Raised to the lips, by means of the hands. Carried.

No need to rehearse all of this to feel the con-fidence which the bowl inspires, warm and instinc-tual. Physical, immediately perceptible. The bowl always fits the hand, more or less, and it always has the measure of the stomach. When the *Bardo Thödol*, the *Tibetan Book of the Dead*, gives as its unit of time for a prayer or a ceremony, 'the length of a meal', it means this: the interval of a stomach, a bowlful of time.

Permanently available, adapted to our human scale, a sort of open cave, a warm receptacle, the bowl is self-evidently the most maternal and reassuring of objects. It is not without reason that the monks of the Buddha's community got rid of everything except the begging bowl. It served them in a sense as a proxy house. For the bowl seems – notwithstanding the archaic power of things maternal – quite devoid of threat. An entirely rounded breast, entirely smooth, seem-ingly anterior to all conflict, all division. Which is why there is something so immutable about the bowl. History may trick it out in various materials

– in wood or terracotta; in glazed stoneware or in plastic; in ceramic adorned with the Christian name of your girlfriend; in shiny aluminium for hikes in the mountains, or in earthenware for life on the farm – but all of them share a family likeness: placid and welcoming.

It is a powerful thing, whose power is linked to its frailty. Which is why it is a thing of thresholds, of beginnings and endings. Baby's bowl, old man's bowl. Morning bowl (cereal, tea, milk, coffee, porridge), evening bowl (soup, broth, herb tea), this thing is present when life starts up and gathers strength, and when it wanes and grows languid. In between, busy with living, you put it away and forget about it.

On this particular evening, I fall asleep and dream of books that resemble bowls full of words.

Paperclip

I retrieve it by chance, hidden in a fold of leather, while groping to find a pen at the bottom of my briefcase. It must have fallen out of a file. Or else it's been stuck there for ages, caught in that groove where a bit of dust, or a scrap of paper, or an elastic band always get stuck. An intact paperclip, metallic and svelte, dry, clean.

This thing inspires sympathy. From where I am standing, at least. You may of course feel differently. Sympathy for paperclips is not universal. It's merely my point of view – but what other view can I take of the world? And you, do you know what it feels like to be a spider? Or a giraffe? Or a coathanger? Or to be your neighbour? You may think you do. But in fact, you do not. Not at all. And neither do I. So, I am allowed to feel sympathy for paperclips without anyone making a fuss about it.

What is sympathetic about a paperclip? The ingenious bend? The smooth, light, metallic neatness? The little triangle at one end, so perfectly adapted to the tip of the tongue? The temptation to contort and dismember it? The fact that it is just a small thing of no consequence? I would rescue the paperclip for the category of 'unassuming things'. It is cousin to the pin, but far gentler. You can't prick yourself. It makes no holes in your papers. The paperclip harms nothing. It has neither the brutality of the staple, nor the intrusive character of other fastening devices.

The paperclip belongs to the category of things taken for granted. Which is why it pleases me so much. You could never accuse a paperclip of showing off! It does nothing to get noticed. In fact, it never does get noticed. Nobody could describe it as indispensable. It performs its function, as required, within its limits, doggedly. Dependable. Not brilliant, but dependable.

Revelatory, too, albeit with characteristic modesty. Not every epoch, nor every society, has had paperclips. The existence of the paperclip presupposes machine tools capable of working a type of metallic thread, perfectly uniform, supple, flexible; it also presupposes a world of documents, of sheets of paper needing to be fastened to each other, a world of offices, meetings, files, office staff, office accessories, office furniture. The birth of the paperclip must date from the beginning of the last century. And the signs are that it is not going to live for ever. Quite possibly, in the not so distant future, we shall witness the passing of the paperclip.

And with the death of the paperclip, we shall have lost one of the figures of Eros. This little twist of metal, that gathers and fastens papers together, puts one in mind (in its small way) of what Freud meant by Eros. Not sexuality exactly, and much less orgasm. Rather the power that binds without paralysing. The strength which resists dispersal of energy. The life force which counters entropy. In its modest and metallic way, the paperclip does all of these things. Like the bowl, albeit very differently, it offers containment.

I recall a particular moment. A while ago I found some old files of mine, going back to my youth. They had been in storage in the country for some years, in a damp house. Over the course of time, the paperclips had rusted. And when I slipped them off, they left a brown stain and indentation on the papers, and rough specks of rust on my fingers. But they had not loosened their grip. They had held fast, and acquitted themselves, despite the years and the rust.

For its way of doing what has to be done, without show or complaint (hard to imagine the revolt of the paperclips), in the shadows, indifferent to intrigue and honours, anonymous and utile, neither heroic nor rash, but loyal and earnest – for these reasons the paperclip is also a figure of ethics.

Remote Control

at home, end of the day

It has started to get surprisingly hot for the time of year. The weather is in exaggerated mood. Impossible to do anything. Impossible to string two ideas together. Nothing for it but a drip-feed of television . . . Fortunately, the remote control is to hand, having taken up residence on the sofa. A weird object. Inconceivable for generations previous to ours. Awkward even for us: a short plastic stick, covered in buttons, remotely controlling more functions than its end-users can commit to memory.

You know as well as I do that there is no mystery here: this thing contains batteries, printed circuits, wires and cables, an entire paraphernalia of manufactured parts, explicable down to the tiniest detail, technologically self-righteous. It was planned, conceived, discussed, tested and manufactured. Distributed and sold. Extended warranty. You are kept well informed: instructions, a throng of functions from the multitude of keys, sometimes with other tactile gimmicks thrown in.

Despite all of which, it remains a thing of magic, a psychic thing, a thing of sorcery. You aim it, it lights up and then goes dark; it changes channels, discs, radio stations; it increases the sound, lowers the sound, cuts all sound; changes the sequencing, the lighting, the setting. Without your having to get up or make any movement, without having to go and touch the buttons over there – not exactly far away, but elsewhere all the same, mounted in some other box. Making things happen from a distance, totally effective, as if by pure will. As in dreams, as in spells, curses, witches' brews. With the suddenness of thought that can summon phantoms, and with the terrible precision of silent wishes.

And, equally, with the same hit or miss quality! For the trick doesn't work every time. You point, you press, and . . . nothing happens. You repeat the gesture, exactly the same, and this time yes, it obeys. Which is precisely what convinces us that magic is involved.

Of all our electronic and post-electronic things, the remote control is the most archaic. It connects us back to a time when our wishes became facts. Of which our earliest infancy – never entirely the past – was proof, when we thought we knew that desire was sufficient. No sooner imagined than realised: the enemy is routed, the breast appears, unpleasure is banished, satisfaction is assured. Without delay. Without detours. Without effort. Without thinking. Without limit. With nothing to fear, and even less to forego.

Each of us must learn to renounce the omnipotence of our desires. It is a long process, in part painful. Necessarily arduous, involving trial and error, and only partially successful. Despite which, if we are even vaguely adult, this bereavement was over and done with years ago. We are even told that such is the condition of our having a viable rapport with reality.

Things are what resist our desires. That could be a minimal but acceptable definition: those realities not immediately at the disposal of our will are referred to as things. Kant knew as much: 'My thought imposes no requirement upon things.' Reality imposes – on whoever would wish to modify it – indirections, hard work, an indefinite series of physical actions subject to constraint and limitation.

The remote control kisses goodbye to all that.

It re-immerses us in the imaginary world where to wish is to act. It gloriously confirms us in thinking of ourselves as masters of the world. It shows us, demonstrably, that we are capable of realising our desires from a distance, without moving. We may have to press this button or that button, and in a sense therefore to act, however minimally. But this hardly qualifies as an action in the full sense. The thumb is a direct extension of the thought, which it prolongs in a single unobtrusive gesture of approbation.

The remote control succeeds where prayers failed. Pick up your remote control. Make it lower the room temperature, or turn it up if need be. Now cause night to fall, the dawn to come up; make your partner take off her clothes and put them back on quick as a flash; now make the cupboards fill up (with food, clothes, household linen, CDs, soaps, perfumes). Now find the button for peace on earth, for an end to poverty, for universal prosperity, for mutual respect, for sustainable development, for human dignity. For eternal life.

Keys

In the world of things, nothing much has been happening for several days. There they are, still but unresponsive, shut off. Mute. I can get nothing out of them. However intently I scrutinise them. Nothing. Complete indifference. I contemplate the bathroom. Stalemate. No way of squeezing the ghost of an idea out of the sponges, or the toothbrush. The dustbin is as indifferent as Rimbaud's drunken boat to all the 'Flemish wheat or English cottons' it is carrying. My plan of enquiry into the nature of things is unworkable. It is stupid, stalled at the outset. The only solution: give it up, and put an end to this temporary folly.

Just as I am leaving the house, impossible to find my keys anywhere. They are not in my study, not in the bedroom, not in the pockets of my jacket. Not in the kitchen (why would I have put them in the kitchen?). If this continues I am going to be late. I must find them this instant. The set of duplicate keys is locked out of reach. Typical example of the subterfuge of keys: the key to the drawer in my desk where the duplicate set is kept was beginning to wear out; so I had a new copy made yesterday, stupidly locking the drawer, so that the (old) key of the drawer together with the (new) duplicate are on the same bunch of keys I have mislaid. You understand the problem.

Finally I spot the stray keys on the mantel-piece. Naturally I examine them with gratitude and renewed attention. What a weird thing a key is! A few bits of metal, notches, grooves, milled edges, like a graph, or a mountain range against the horizon. A thing that jangles; fairly ugly, graceless. Yet so vital despite everything, so imbued with power, so indispensable: the *sine qua non* for entering and leaving, for inhabiting, for driving, working, travelling.

The solitary key, first of all. Straight, tapered. Made of steel, or metal of some kind, evidently. (No such thing as a floppy key, or a key made of perishable material). Of uncommon hardness, and uncommon solitude. A notched and obstinate silence, turned in upon itself. The key possesses all the principal attributes of power: enigmatic, solitary, indifferent to its own isolation. Devoid of sense, and likewise of any intrinsic purpose: look at an abandoned key, a key no longer in use. A pitiful sight, like a dead fish. A superfluous piece of metal, its weight a mere burden.

For a key to live, it has to open and shut things. To afford entry, to deny entry. Entry to what? No matter what, whether a house, a safe, a cupboard, a car, a desk. All keys, brass or steel, iron or aluminium, share this concentrated power: to make something open, or to keep something closed. The key carries around, in portable form, this power over the door. No one else, unless they are in possession of an identical key, can open it or close it.

The keys of the car (of the motorbike, of the scooter) represent this power at its most explosive: the key engages, starts up, sets in motion. In it are condensed all the possibilities of propulsion, of travel, of speed. A car without a key is even more abandoned than a key without a lock: the absence of a mere bit of metal leaves all this machinery inert, useless, forsaken.

I think somewhat furtively of all the keys I have ever received or given. A sign of trust and, when they are without strict utility or purpose, a token of love. When we give a set of keys, or are given them, or when we return them, or take them back again, might this be how love is measured out, between lovers?

More accurate to say that, for lovers, each is the other's key. A matter of precise adjustment, exactness of contour. Nothing to do with complementarity, in fact. The key does not complete the lock. It opens the lock, it activates it, lends its power to it. The lover gives the other back to himself or herself, to the fullness of which he or she is capable. With that enigmatic hardness proper to love.

Love once fled is either a closed door or a door impossible to close. Think of that: of our loves as a bunch of keys, each in turn opening or closing, not our whole being perhaps (there is no such thing as our whole being), but this or that portion. A drawer here, a district there, a door, a vehicle.

It's time I let myself out of the house.

Sunglasses

café terrace,
morning, in the city

The heat-wave has started to abate. For three days, violent storms have succeeded one another almost without interval. This morning, the weather is notably less sultry. But the brilliance of the light is of an almost disturbing intensity, the sky utterly clear. The rains have washed everything, including the light itself. Not a mote of dust as far as the eye can see. Only this harsh clarity, without a trace of mist. It is rare to be able to see the world thus. So rare that it makes us realise what a lifeless monochrome we usually struggle inside.

I rarely wear sunglasses, except when I am in the South, and in high summer. But this morning, if I am to take my coffee on the terrace and read the newspaper, there is no alternative. In the reflection of the window, I see with my own eyes that I can no longer see my own eyes. In this game of hide and seek, this tiny but absolute act of dissimulation, lies the special power of dark glasses. Which may explain why they are so timelessly chic. The phenomenon is unusual: throughout the entire world, used by all social groups and classes, worn by every generation, these objects persist in seeming somehow élitist. They are the most stubbornly élitist of ordinary, everyday things. Their distinction has nothing to do with their utility value, which is humdrum. Sunglasses protect from the sun's glare, but this function is entirely secondary.

What counts with sunglasses, in the first place, is that they transport you instantly to another world. A green world. Or a yellow world. Or blue. Or pink. Or brown, or beige. Variously coloured, variously distinct from our first world. No diffusion, no sharply contrasting colours. This second world is peculiar on all counts: rigorously identical to the first (you recognise people, places, things; nothing in effect surprises you), yet totally different (colour of sky, nuances of light, outlines of things – no scene is untransformed).

It does not take a philosopher to conclude that the world of appearances is a function of our vision.

Things are not as we see them, despite which, for us, they can only be as we see them. Impossible to see beyond our seeing. And yet sunglasses change what is seen. Filters of colour, they distort and they transform. And what if we tried to dispense with our usual ways of seeing, just as we would remove a pair of sunglasses? How would we set about it? By blinding ourselves? Or merely by considering the world from another angle?

There is something else about sunglasses, more unsettling and more fundamental. They conceal our eyes. Like portable masks, but in reverse (since the mask, traditionally, disguises everything except the eyes). To hide one's gaze constitutes a singular form of withdrawal, a distancing effect which yet creates intimations of menace and kindles an unspecified distrust. It is not for nothing that generals, movie stars, Mafia bosses, aesthetes and torturers are represented – and portray themselves, so to speak, collusively – as wearing dark glasses. A black world in this case, for the sun has no place in these scenarios. Such spectacles serve only to mask the gaze, indefinitely. Perhaps the motley crowd who deploy them share a certain taste for secrecy and for the theatre of cruelty.

Evidently the various attributes of sunglasses

converge in this opacity, which brings to a stumbling halt the look of the other. The chic or élitist aspect connects with this distancing effect, this emancipation of the look from any expression in the eyes, this air of 'I am watching you but I am shielded, hidden, and you cannot decipher me'. Power and cruelty are likewise implicated in any gaze that shirks reciprocity, that refuses to be looked upon in turn.

You are aware of a gaze being trained upon you, but you are unable to look it in the eye. You no longer feel directly the presence of the other. You merely presume it. You postulate its existence behind the opaque screen, but you do not experience it. And this presence in turn comes to mean power or authority, is formidable in proportion to its withdrawal. And it keeps avoiding you. By masking the eyes, and only the eyes, black glasses reflect back negatively what the open look characteristically allows: instinctive recognition, transparency, enlisting the goodwill of the other.

Let us place side by side, in thought only, a woman wearing the veil according to Islamic law and a nudist wearing sunglasses. In the former case all is concealed, as a rule, even the face; only the eyes are offered to view. In the case of the nudist, only the eyes are shielded from the look of the other. Which of the two can be considered as the more effectively concealed? And why? This could provide debate for long winter evenings.

And I have forgotten to read my newspaper.

Alarm Clock

at home, early morning

A loud rending noise. The peaceful course of the blood brutally interrupted. Like when you cut yourself peeling vegetables, or shaving: nothing serious, no real pain, but the flesh opened, the surface broken. When the alarm clock goes off, it feels like that. A rapid succession of noises, high-pitched, strident, on a single note. Pins and needles inside your skull.

From what I can make out (with one eye open), it says 6.46 a.m. If the alarm goes off at 6.46 a.m. there has to be a reason. I must try to deduce the reason. No success, not yet, not by a long chalk, not immediately . . . Oh yes, I remember. I have to catch a train. Right now.

As far as alarm clocks go, given the difficulties I have in paying attention to them, I have tried more or less everything: the tick-tock variety that

- 37 -

prevent sleep, the luminous sort that dazzle you in the dark, the musical kind that don't go off, the radio clocks that induce panic about the state of the world, the compact-disc clocks that are so confusing. In the end, I prefer to stay with the high-pitched emergency alarm built into my watch. It does not try to tell the news or play music, nor is it interested in being on intimate terms with the client. Shrillness is all its cry, and nothing but shrillness, boring its way into my tympanum until my eyes are opened. Violence, naked and undisguised.

There is no 'natural' waking, except when waking occurs unaccompanied, of its own accord, at the end of sleep, as if it were sleep's overflow. Fulfilment and repudiation, the return of day. The dawn of light. Recomposition of the world. Little by little, imperceptibly. But to be awakened at a predetermined hour is a violent intrusion. Fairly commonplace, I know. Useful, I'm prepared to concede. None of which diminishes the violence in question.

What drags you out of sleep, and thence out of bed, and presently out of your home, is a powerful social mechanism for co-ordination. The alarm goes off because you must go to work, must wake the children for school, must take the train, take the underground, take the plane, check into the factory, arrive at the office, be where you are expected, where others claim you and survey you. All of which requires a vast control of activities and trajectories. A social discipline ever more clenched, ever more calibrated.

In times past an entire social group – a village, an army – was summoned by the tolling of a bell or the blowing of a horn. Such occasions were rare, and human dwellings close together. The history of modern societies – their birth, their evolution – is the progressive ascendancy of clock-time over human lives. The world we see about us is the result of an immense synchronisation.

When was the first mechanical timepiece in-stalled in the town square, at the heart of things? And with what effects – in China, in Africa, in the Orient? How did they set about capturing all these individual entities in the mesh of their network? So many diverse individuals, so many distinct peoples, with their disparate rhythms, how were they all compelled?

It seems to us a self-evident matter that the alarm goes off, that the news begins at a fixed hour, that the bus or train leaves or arrives at thirty-two minutes past the hour or twenty-seven minutes to the hour. How many centuries of knocking into shape were required, how many slowly domesticated generations, to arrive at this result, with every back bowed to the discipline of the clock? Slowly but surely, things for telling the time attached themselves to us physically. At first we saw from afar the great clock in the market square. Then at home we watched the clock on the mantelpiece, the clock in the kitchen, followed by the clock on the bedside table. Then the rich started to wear pocket watches, which they would remove from their fobs, from time to time, with a childishly avid gesture, almost of wonder. And finally the watch latched itself on to all our wrists, the world over, in every latitude, on every continent. Nowadays in quartz, in digital form, displaying the very seconds.

It marks each instant of the day – travel, work, play – strapped to us and strapping us down. The watch holds body and soul entirely in bondage to the observance of a temporality that is cramped and demarcated. To put on your watch in the morning is to don a cape of carefully woven obligations. The watch yields the exact avoirdupois of time, which of itself weighs – of course – nothing.

Time, which wakes me up, is in principle utterly reliable. Set by remote control, from a centre which corrects its possible variations. Never too fast or too slow. Time is always on time. Is there any difference between our watches and those electronic tags imposed on prisoners serving out their term at home? Yes, there is. I can take off my watch and enter some of those worlds where time's pressure is low: the world in which I make love, the world in which I submerge myself in water, the world in which I go to sleep.

There are grounds for howling at our universal manipulation. Is it not baleful that so many things in our lives are effectively remote-controlled? Well, at least our gift for complaint is not controlled. It is still we who decide whether to moan or not.

Salt Cellar

canteen, lunchtime

This week there is so much work that I have become incapable of taking things in. The same goes for people. There are times when I become merely a function of what I am doing. When what needs to get done gets done. But then I am no longer in a position to attend to all the rest – things, places, people. Today, for example, surrounded by the hubbub of a lunchtime canteen, eating hastily. I register that the salad lacks salt; but the salt cellar is not on the table. Normally, it should be on the table. Which is why I have now noticed it, because it is not there, in its usual place: hovering, in the background. Being available, while knowing how to make itself discreet. Its job is simply to be there. Just in case. On the off-chance.

Whenever your food tastes insipid, you reach for the salt cellar. With a glance, with your hand, absent-mindedly. It is forever within reach. Always present and correct, and as soon forgotten. Or if not, you get irritated and have to seek it out. Sometimes far afield, at the other end of the table. In other words, it is a thing that comes and goes. Without steady employment. Nevertheless, single-handedly and permanently on duty. To be reliable is its responsibility, not your problem. All you ask of it is to be there, ready to play its part. Whatever the hour, without warning. The SOS of flavour. Perpetually on call.

Innumerable other things are required to be permanently on call. Evidently, being required to be permanently on call is an essential attribute of things. But the salt cellar involves more than this. It has been, since time immemorial, an index of civilisation. Think of the history of salt. The prehistory of salt : deposits form in the cavities of rocks, visible on the surface, which hunter-gatherers notice and then taste. Ancient forms of transportation: feluccas, the slow progress of a semi-magical commodity. Classical entrepôts: salt-tax collectors, and at the far end of the cellar the pig being salted away for winter in the salting-tub. You suspect that there must be entire libraries on the subject of salt, its trade routes, its successive roles in human evolution. This vast story, of craziness and conflict, of science and trade and expansion, of rationality and flavour, culminates in the absolute banality of the salt cellar, at one end of the table, on its little tin-plated display rack.

What was a rarity, something extremely precious, an enigma, is become entirely commonplace. Universal, practically without value. No restaurant, even the poorest, charges you for the use of the salt cellar. A sign of civilisation: the integration into everyday existence of an ancient rarity. It is so entirely part of the self-evidence of our common life, that we have lost even the memory of its formerly exceptional character.

The salt cellar, to fulfil its purpose, is usually turned the wrong way, upside down, momentarily. Not too much! A tiny quantity suffices. Just enough to blend in, to stir, to dissolve. Just enough to ensure that it is not confused with its opposite (sugar), from which it is almost indistinguishable to the naked eye. Look again at these attributes. Something rendered commonplace. Used in small quantities. Well mixed in. Not to be confused with what seems, at first sight, to be exactly the same (stupidity). Does all of this not suggest, precisely, the characteristics of human intelligence?

The war against blandness is a strange combat. And the salt cellar is a modern figure for what used to be called, so long ago, the human soul. The salt of the earth has come to mean anyone at all.

Pressed for time, I look at my watch mechanically.

Drawer

Since yesterday, it has started to become seriously cold. A manner of speaking, perhaps. Others would say it is cool, if that. Do they appreciate the extremities to which we who are sensitive to the cold are condemned, in temperate countries? Scrutinising mail-order catalogues for winter clothing at the first sign of a cloud; rummaging for leather gloves and woollen socks at the fall of the first autumn leaf. Each drop in temperature noted as a source of anxiety, a further step towards a state of numbness, of being chilled to the bone, chained to the fireside, on pain of complete shutdown of vital functions.

I shall be wearing a scarf from now onwards, for the rest of the year; that is settled. My scarves are all in a drawer, in a chest of drawers, in my bedroom. I go to fetch one. And all at once – how shall

I put it? – the drawer is *there*, in front of me. All the in-between bits are merely a blur. The drawer is quite distinct, dense with self-presence, detached from its surroundings. Which is always how this experience occurs: a particular thing suddenly materialises before me. I cannot know which thing in advance. I cannot know why this one in particular has interposed itself so abruptly.

I open and close the drawer several times. I see my scarves appear, disappear, reappear, re-disappear. I lapse into an old stupor, one of the postures of childhood. How can there be a space inside space? A cordoned-off place, a world *b* inserted into the usual world *a*? A second universe. And then another, and another still, as many worlds as there are drawers, all recessed within the visible and known universe.

We know that the folds in the garment of this world are countless. Grottoes, crypts, caves, houses, sheds, cupboards, boxes, books, newspapers . . . A thousand spaces are hidden, reserved, open to those who are able to enter, otherwise unknown. The drawer belongs to this family. From which it is also set apart. This being its singularity: that a drawer slides open and slides closed.

When you open the door of a cupboard, you can immediately peer inside, inspect and scrutinise its contents. The cupboard is a room given over to certain things, on a reduced scale. The drawer functions differently. It offers up its contents to your gaze when you draw it from its housing, while at the same time remaining itself partially housed. If it is removed entirely, a drawer becomes a mere box. Its enigmatic charm, as drawer, resides in this to-and-fro quality, this sliding by which it offers up its contents to your eyes and fingers, without quite leaving its cave, and afterwards reverts to the hermetic condition of a sealed object.

What the drawer suggests is this: the existence of a world bristling with the unseen. Behind its façade, and capable of appearing and disappearing at will, are a series of other spaces, with wildly varying contents, whether jumbled up or ranged in order, multi-coloured or monochrome. A universe of strata, without end. Multi-storied. Subdivided and parcelled out into plots, each rapidly offered and as rapidly withdrawn from view.

The drawer as a paradigm is replicated elsewhere in daily life. The pull-down menus of computers, the operations of memory, the exegesis of hidden meanings. Hypertext is one gigantic drawer: behind every word lie other possibilities, cross-references, entire encyclopaedias, an infinity of interlocking compartments. Our mental life itself functions partly on this model. I often think of my head as stocked with drawers. Rapidly opening and closing different universes, dossiers, ideas, registers. Parallel worlds, which only communicate with each other when asked to do so. In actual fact, our mental drawers shut very badly. They are not watertight. Fortunately so?

Ultimately, the experiment of this book consists in supposing that each thing encountered is a drawer. With a bit of luck, from time to time I manage to open one. I never know in advance what it will contain. Nothing, perhaps. Perhaps traces of something I am not able to understand. Or something clsc? And here I feel for the first time a small measure of apprehension. What is this story on which I have embarked?

Scarf

in a café, beginning of winter

I put on a scarf before going out, for the first time
this year. A moment of annual recurrence. I now
feel reassured, confident of not feeling the wind,
of not 'catching cold' – an old maternal fear,
which I have often mocked in myself, and which
remains embedded despite everything.

There is something about the scarf that suggests another dimension. But what? In the world
of things, clothes occupy a place apart. In the
shops they are mere things, asleep amongst other
things. More supple perhaps, more responsive,
but captive nonetheless in the banal domain of
commodity. At home, in the closet, or the wardrobe,
or the cupboard, or the drawer, clothes are still
things, of course, but they are replete with memories and with the occasions of the body. This shirt
means that long walk in Normandy. This T-shirt

recalls Patmos, that jacket says New York, this lumber-jacket means Seoul (commodore-class memories). Or it evokes my cousin, my brother-in-law, my neighbours (steerage-class memories). It doesn't matter which. The article retains the patina of time; you may not be thinking of what it has been through, but it bears a family likeness to a particular moment in the past.

Once it has been worn, an item of clothing is no longer distinguishable from the body wearing it. It prolongs the body, marries it, transforms it, inhabits it, supports it. In contact with our skin, and in movement with our movements, clothes make it impossible for us to think of them as mere things undifferentiated from other things.

We live our clothes as though they were alive. Your trousers do the walking. Your jacket extends its arm. Your shirt moves briskly or sits down. Never do you have the impression that clothes merely follow – like a shell or a lifeless burden – wherever your gestures and movements lead. Except in particular instances (an overcoat that is too heavy, a pullover that is too small, a pair of jeans that are too tight), we do not feel as if we carry and stretch and transport clothes on our shoulders, arms and legs. They share your mobility to the point of blending with your actions.

Impossible, under these circumstances, to think of an article of clothing as a thing. What it crucially lacks is inertia. Things as such are immobile, incapable of movement. Virtually all things. In recent times, of course, machines were invented that are capable of movement. But would you think of your clothes as motorised? No. What causes them to elude the common rule of things is the suppleness of their mobility, its spontaneous character, its half-life, at the boundary of animate and inanimate.

It is for this same reason that clothes exist in a particular relation to time past. They are integrated into the body's memory, an accumulation of physical acts and sensations, a sequence of gestures linked each to each, whose mutuality owes nothing to consciousness or the deductions of logic. The body has lived through a particular moment with a particular garment, and it silently remembers the fact.

My scarf, for me as for many other people, is linked umbilically to my mother. Here I am, getting ready for school. It is still dark outside. 'Don't forget your muffler.' My mother still says 'muffler' (*cache-col*). I only came to understand the word much later. At the time, I was quite unaware that it had to do with hiding the neck (*cacher le cou*) – to me it was simply a '*cachcol*'. I would fetch it, she would tie it round my neck, and off I would go with my satchel.

I do not think of these things in any clear and conscious fashion each time I put on a scarf. Such thoughts are present in concealed form, in the filigree of accompanying gestures, and visible only under a certain light. How does so much life manage to lurk within such ordinary things? It suffices to take hold of one, at random, for entire worlds to be uncovered.

The scarf, moreover, is one of the simplest of garments. No couture. No cutting-out necessary. Nothing but a length of material, wool or silk, whatever. Placed around the neck and either knotted or worn open, according to choice. All in all, a bit like memory itself.

Streetlamp

one evening, chez 'l'Oiseau'

When I am staying with the woman I love, which is nearly always (the rest of the time she stays with me), I see a streetlamp from her window. It is an old streetlamp, with a long, thin, fluted column, topped by a sort of metal hat shaped like a bell. The bulb is protected by glass and points downwards, held in place from above. The shape of the thing is suggestive of London, or northern Europe in general, rather than France. An outmoded variety, relatively rare in Paris, standing outlined against the trees in the square just below. One can see it from the bed, through the window.

Why does this streetlamp have such an effect upon me? Is it the slightly strange and even foreign aspect of the thing, which makes me feel that I am not quite in Paris? Or is it perhaps the lamp's habit of evoking mist, and the way its solitude conjures up images of the inevitable pea-souper, and the muffled sound of horses' hooves in the distance, as of a late cab passing? Or perhaps it is the yellow light – very yellow, bordering on orange – which I find somehow reassuring when night has fallen. It must be all of these things at once.

I have a special weakness for the way in which it alone is the bearer of light amidst the surrounding indifference. There is something of the small lighthouse about its deportment. Impervious to all opinion. Whether anyone is passing or not – and generally in this square there is no one – it shines bravely forth, in so far as it is able. And when occasionally there is a passer-by, its demeanour remains unchanged. Always reliable.

In which sense the streetlamp resembles her. She is not from these parts either, nor really even from northern Europe. She too corresponds to a human type endowed with old-fashioned elegance. She too persists in giving light without worrying who is there. She too stands forth in a reassuring and joyous solitude.

It's not that I am in love with a streetlamp. But I give thanks to it, where it stands under the bedroom window, for having made me understand, and allowed me to express, or at least to glimpse, how this species of love exists by granting the solitude of the other. Very near and solid, and light of step too, and as if permanently on.

Window. Light. Curtain.

Exercise Book

chez 'l'Oiseau',
a different evening

Each day it gets dark a little sooner. For many people this is a cause of regret. I have no desire to go against collectively shared emotions, but this nocturnal veil, which nightly enlarges the circle of its hours, has a reassuring effect on me. The shadows soothe me. I greet their encroachment as a blissful relief.

There is something hard-edged about daytime and its glare, its commotion; one has to be on one's guard, always ready to react. Things themselves, in this light, look as if somehow grounded. Fixed, congealed inside the stupor of the day. Their contours are flattened, their forms stilled, their presence is in hiding. As soon as it gets dark, things begin to open up and their ways of being come to the fore. As if in darkness they become more confident. More at ease.

At least it seems so to me. I realise that I am merely projecting these impressions on to things. That things are in themselves neither fugitive nor forthcoming. But, as I have said before, I can only see through my own eyes and think with my own head. Never will I convince myself entirely that the day is other than a foreign country, and night other than a house of refuge. And in the night, if we want to put pen to paper, what we need is an exercise book.

The exercise book is an old-fashioned object, a product of the industrial age. It has nothing to do with wax tablets and parchment on the one hand, nor with screens and keyboards on the other. Its singularity consists in its being a gathering of blank pages, bound together. It is a thing-receptacle, destined to preserve a sequence of handwritten traces. An archaic thing, therefore, and perhaps doubly so. Firstly, in the history of technologies of writing: even if it continues to exist for a long time to come, the notebook belongs to the past; the computer threatens it, the electronic pocketbook begins to ridicule it. Secondly, in the history of the individual: wherever you go, the notebook preserves an indestructible link backwards to our childhood.

The exercise book in fact reeks of school. The lines, the squares, the margins, the anxiety of application, the fear of error, of untidiness – of making a mess, of making a mistake. It is one of the principal instruments of control, concentration and discipline in the child's apprenticeship to the social norms that govern the symbolic order.

Let us not underestimate, then, this bound gathering of blank pages. Whether sewn or glued, or both, or spiral bound. Squared or lined or blank. The format varies, the number of pages likewise. What remains constant, however, is this gathered ensemble of paper waiting to be written upon. Something quite distinct from the loose sheet, and from the notepad, whose destiny is to see its pages dispersed. The exercise book, on the contrary, brings together and preserves an itinerary of writing, a sequence of signs spread out over a succession of time. Exercise books, registers (hotel, shipping, trade logs) share the same purpose, of binding handwritten traces together in due order.

The thickness of the exercise book partakes of the thickness of an actual book, the thickness of time itself; it cannot yield itself entirely at a single glance. It reveals itself little by little, page by page, if not line by line. Whence the fascination, the vertigo induced by brand-new exercise books, on which nothing has yet been inscribed. So many possibilities lie in waiting, more numerous than can be dreamt of.

To cover the pages of a notebook, likewise, is to see a multitude of possibilities recede. A single text is committed to paper, line after line: as plural as one might wish it to be, yet single in spite of everything.

I abhor self-referentiality – cinema about cinema, the play within the play, novels about the novel, laughing cow cheese in a laughing cow box – so I will pass over in silence the thing with which or on which I am writing these lines. There are enough blank pages left to keep me going. So much the better. Outside it is dark. Better still. The street-lamp shines on. Happiness here and now.

Boiler

at home, winter morning

This time there can be no mistake. It really is cold.
The thing I most fear, deep down. I can take or
leave the rest – discomfort, ugliness, even hunger.
If I have to. It's true that I like comfort, beauty and
almost everything edible. You too, no? But I could
do without them at a pinch, I could endure minimal conditions. But not as regards temperature.
When the temperature drops, a sense of acute
danger registers in the grain of my being. In the
event of a freeze I risk irreversible shrinkage. If
the cold is allowed to install itself, the air to congeal, I can sense my whole body, and perhaps
more than my body, withdrawing into a dead
zone, curling up in a slow agony of immobility,
worse than extinction itself.

I check the boiler. Just to reassure myself that it
is in good order. That it is still there. That there

are no leaks, no abnormalities. No weird noises. Humming away as usual. In other words, magic as usual. For I know nothing about boiler maintenance. I am incapable of repairing the boiler; I am incapable of servicing it, or of cleaning it. As far as I am concerned, and as far as you are concerned perhaps, the boiler belongs to the order of things mysterious. I simply verify that it is well and truly there, present and correct. Faithful but functional. Pulsing and roaring away.

Boilers, even seen from close up, remain hidden. They are usually located somewhere out of the way, relegated to a basement, or a shed, or the laundry room, or the box-room, or to the corner of a kitchen, or one end of a bathroom. When you sidle up and contemplate them, they still shy away from view. Smooth, cubic, shiny, equipped with barely a dial or a lever, just a few knobs. The essential is withdrawn from view.

They are banished for good reasons. Boilers are noisy, they sometimes smell, they give off effluvia of fuel or oil. Some are too bulky not to find themselves condemned to basements and dingy nooks. The boiler belongs to the family of vital things that are concealed. Things that are always underneath, or behind, or down below, or inside other things; which themselves remain invisible and yet ensure the smooth running of the whole show. Pipes, cables, wires, turbines, filters, generators, myriads of things that enable the circulation of air, water, energy; that transform, heat, propel, evacuate, recycle – unceasingly and without intermission.

Things such as veins, arteries, organs. Such as the *élan vital* itself. The boiler is the dusty heart, the obstinate machinery which keeps life circulating around the house, in winter, when outdoors the night turns blue. From time to time, we should give thought to these multitudes of hidden things, with conscious gratitude. Not too often. To forget about them is normal too. No one walks very far who ponders their cardiac hydraulics.

Returning to my workroom, my work table, my armchair, the illuminated screen of my computer – these things I need if I am to retain my sense of warmth during the winter darkness ahead – it occurs to me that the boiler is a fridge in reverse. By devising both, we have extended our franchise over nature in opposite directions. Opposite or complementary? Opposite or identical?

Questions I

The experiment has lasted three months. I have frequently been on the point of abandoning it, as an absurd and pathetic endeavour. In spite of which, I persist. Some impulse stronger than this conviction has carried me along thus far. At moments I have the impression of being sent on a mission. Impossible to say precisely what kind of mission. Equally impossible simply to quit.

Why, for example, when talking about things, do I start to talk about myself? I detest intimate journals. Memoirs, autobiographies, confessions – they all bore me. In spite of which, here we are on the subject of things, and a narrator emerges endowed with the full range of my personal manias and foibles. Can it be that talking about things involves exhibiting the bits and pieces of self that adhere to their substance? Is it possible to do otherwise, or are we hopelessly entangled with things?

So much for the pure object facing the pure subject. The subject, alas, cannot be purged of individual particularities, the paraphernalia of penchants, tastes, talents and oddities. To shake them off requires too much violence. To obtain a cleansed awareness, neutralised, stripped of character traits, reduced to its transcendent purity, one needs to have trampled one's past underfoot, made mincemeat of one's emotions, eviscerated one's guts, eradicated all distinguishing traits – indeed, everything that composes an actual identity. The result of such an operation: pure artifice – a rational being confronting an object world as abstract as himself.

What I have learnt from this experiment, in its early stages, is the exact contrary: that in order to approach the reality, the multifariousness and inexhaustible singularity of individual existences, one must embrace the anecdotal, the discontinuous, the shifts of perspective implied by this permanent and inextricable interlocking of things and people, people and things. One must defer to the unforeseeable interactions of variable subjects and discontinuous or singular objects.

In these waters I am guided by two pilots, Montaigne and Nietzsche. Neither of whom can think without talking about himself. Their singularity is everywhere present and perceptible. Not that they ever talk about themselves for the sake of effusion. They have no interest in placing their lives under our scrutiny. On the contrary: they look *with their lives*; they describe and they think *with their lives*. Whence a certain habit, in their writings, of being always in the picture without ever being at its centre, and a manner of tackling things and ideas that is richly indistinct, both unsettled and unsettling. Whence, above all, the bringing into play of a type of subject and a type of object that are neither self-enclosed nor fixed in place, but ceaselessly transforming and reforming themselves. 'There is no continuity of being, whether in ourselves or in things,' wrote Montaigne in the *Apology for Raymond Sebond*. Errancy, fluctuation, discontinuity. And a similar movement to be traced in Nietzsche, clearly.

The image of a cloud may illustrate this subject and object that remain *open* and *mobile*. Although its edges may be blurred and constantly in motion, the cloud remains clearly visible, its whereabouts unambiguous. This floating nomad, of variable geometry, can be travelled through or dispersed. We need to imagine cloud-subjects, endowed with the usual characteristics (child-bearing, language-using, political animals, etc.), interacting with cloud-objects, endowed with different properties, some of which are still poorly understood. The study of the variable relations between these types of cloud would constitute the science of meteor-osophy. A National Institute for which would publish official bulletins. Whose rate of publication would naturally be irregular.

I have also been asking myself, since the start of this outlandish experiment, what it might mean to scrutinise a bowl or a remote-control handset at a time of fire and bloodshed in so many places and extreme instability elsewhere. And yet. This experiment with things, however personal, must surely have a connection with the turning point at which we now find ourselves.

I have remarked how we live inside a giant patchwork of objects from epochs very distant in time and cultures very distant in space. Although other periods have known conditions similar to ours, none has been exposed to such immoderate juxtaposition, such unprecedented proliferation. Ours is the epoch in which more things are to be encountered on earth than ever before. Each day millions and millions of new things are added to the sum of existing things. And far fewer disappear.

We totter beneath things and they continue to proliferate. But this proliferation is no longer the stuff of dreams. The consumerist fever so universal a few decades ago is over. A few isolated groups, dotted here and there, still work themselves up over the latest product, the newest model. In all moderately developed countries, a brand-new hypermarket is still besieged and people redo their sums, smash the piggy bank, fantasize, renounce, give up on renouncing, borrow, spend, get into debt. As always, the world over. There is little reason for this state of things to end and no reason to howl imprecations. In the rich countries, nonetheless, whose behaviour prefigures how the story will turn out elsewhere, the proliferation of things is pursued in the midst of a more or less universal and loveless indifference. Everyone knows that everything is obtainable, everywhere, and that there is more and more of everything. And we know that the infinite multiplication of things creates problems: storage, transport, refuse, recycling, pollution. The consumer frenzy has abated: things proliferate without arousing enthusiasm or utopian prophecy about their life-saving and happiness-enhancing properties.

This oblivion of things perhaps explains, *a contrario*, the birth of my experiment. It is possible that I say this to reassure or delude myself, but I cannot help thinking that an inverse relation exists between the oblivion which surrounds things and the fact that humanity has entered into a state of upheaval which may lead, quite possibly, to its perdition. Should we not attempt to walk in the direction of things – however pointless or impossible this may seem – towards their silence and their calm? Is it possible that things might provide a haven, a place apart, a resource? For whom? And to what end? Let us investigate. Let us continue to tap at this door.

Do not forget that things reside outside of language. Entirely so. For all that we may give them names and describe them, they remain categorically removed from our world of words. They are likewise beyond truth, absolute strangers to the realm of true and false. Propositions are either true or false, the contents of thought likewise. But things are never thus. Have the consequences of this fairly obvious state of affairs been sufficiently considered? We are creatures of language and reason, net exporters of sentences, seekers after truth, and yet we are surrounded by millions of mute phenomena, things indifferent to all verbal life, resolutely on the outside of our language bubble. And this does not concern us in the least? We behave as if the case were simply otherwise. As if the object world, so close and yet so radically other, did not need to be taken into consideration. To my knowledge, very few philosophers have struck out in this direction, apart from Schopenhauer and Wittgenstein. It is worth asking just how far it is possible to strike out in this direction without losing one's bearings. Given that it involves heading out beyond the point of what is sayable, or thinkable, or available to experience. Beyond this frontier, no one knows what there is. How does one proceed through the land where the wild things are?

On ancient maps, where border country was indicated – the desert margin where routes vanished and landmarks disappeared – the words *Hic sunt leones* used to be inscribed. 'Here are lions'. Meaning savage regions, peopled with forms of life that could not be subjugated. On my map – my map of what? Of my life? My mind? My world? – I would be tempted to write: 'Here are things'. *Hic sunt res*. A posited realm which remains by definition out of reach. Where things are is on the other side of words, on the other shore of our world, which no description can touch. We can only attempt to draw near and capture an echo, obliquely, like a reflection in a looking glass. As in a fable.

It remains to decide how one recognises a thing. We think we know, but the case is not so simple. The word itself is so indeterminate, so all-encompassing, that it insinuates itself everywhere, into all situations. To limit its uses, we have decided that for our present purposes a thing is an object: neither brute matter nor living organism, but a product of human labour, usually inert, and whose purpose can usually be deduced. But this definition reassures us for no more than a few moments. Since there exist a multitude of things whose contours are indeterminate. As if certain things were only approximately things, if you see what I mean. I'm not sure that I do.

Our first encounters were with things possessed of physical density, and which functioned as models, or patterns. The bowl, for example, furnishes the type for all other receptacles. Compress the bowl, deepen it, raise its sides, and you obtain the glass; on the contrary, open it out, flatten it, stretch it, and it becomes a plate. According to size, depth, diameter, you obtain by analogy the entire sequence of domestic receptacles. It approximates to what we mean by a structure. Other things, at the outset of the experiment, perform actions of gathering, or opening, or concealing, or pulsating. But despite their multifariousness of status, their definition is sharp, 'clear and explicit', as Descartes would say.

There must, however, exist things whose place in the scheme is not so easily discerned. Equivocal things, ambiguously intermediate things, things difficult to define at a stroke, impossible to corral within a single definition or function, possessed of more than one identity. Can there really exist double things, triple things, in-between things, whose function is out of step? If so, I do not yet know where they are to be found. I will advance by trial and error.

Trial and Error

THING (sb.), indeterminate designation
for whatever is inanimate.

Littré Dictionary

Bed

at home one morning,
on waking

Do all things qualify as things? Hardly have I opened my eyes than this outlandish question comes into my head. It only succeeds in adding to the state of muddle in which I usually find myself on waking. I know that there are people who, on being thrown suddenly back into the world, pick up smoothly where they left off, without missing a beat. Just like opening the shutters. Like setting foot on the sand again after shouldering the waves. Quickly and painlessly. No trial. No error. No problem.

For me, waking up has always been an intricate business, for as long as I can remember. Mornings are an incomplete world, approximate, unfinished. I have some of the jigsaw, a few clues, but the rest escapes me. Things reconstitute themselves slowly, resume their places one by one, at their own leisure, without my being able to hurry the process, nor bring any of it remotely under my control. I have tried, in the past. It cannot be done. Every morning a dismantled world greets me on waking up. A rough sketch of a world, poorly executed, sometimes quite unrecognisable.

Imagine, for example, that everything were suddenly in black and white, and flattened out, all relief and all colour drained. Or else that you find yourself in an unfamiliar neighbourhood, where the posters, signs, names of shops are written in characters that are indecipherable – in Russian, Greek, Hebrew, Tibetan, Tamil, Chinese. Or that you are walking along a familiar path in thick fog: distances are suddenly unfamiliar, outlines unrecognisable, sounds resonate differently, as if blanketed. In which case you will have a very rough idea of what I call the morning world.

On this particular morning, despite the usual fog, and the shop signs in Tamil, and the film in black and white, I want to get down to business straightaway. So: do all things qualify as things? My bed, for example, everyone would acknowledge to be a thing. In spite of which, when I am stretched out on it, I cannot bring myself to think of it as a thing. I even have the sense that it would take a great deal, an effort of naked will, almost an act of violence, for me to regard this bed on which I am lying as a thing. It is more like a co-ordinate in space: a state of elongation, of lying down. A structuring of the world, rather than an object in the world. The wooden slats or metallic frame are neither here nor there. The bed is the world in a lying-down position, and as such is reducible neither to the mattress nor to the joinery that supports it.

This ambiguity disappears as soon as you consider the bed from outside. When you buy a bed, when you dismantle or mend a bed, when you move house and take your bed with you – pack it, unpack it, measure it, feel the weight of it, move it into position (will it fit through this door? and what about the corridor? and that angle of the stairs?), when you hoover around it or when you change the sheets – then the bed strikes you as a thing, no question. A thing amongst things. However personal, however charged with associations, with emotions, with past and future memories. You are born in one and will die in one; you make love in it, dream in it, take refuge in it, weep in it, go to pieces in it. Every rite of passage takes place within its narrow confines. Yet as soon as we have to move it around or look down on it from above, it reverts abruptly to being a mere thing.

And just as abruptly ceases to be in any sense a mere thing, as soon as you are stretched out on it once more. How can this physical rotation of our verticality, this passage to the horizontal, so entirely transform our perceptions? It is not that the bed suddenly ceases to exist, but that I am no longer able to think of it – simply because I am lying in it or on it – as a thing. Perhaps the bed is only a part-time thing? An intermittent thing, a thing by fits and starts? All the more difficult to understand, in that I can feel it supporting my entire body, from head to toe. My back, backside, legs repose on it and are sustained by it.

Upright and out of bed, I acknowledge categorically that my bed is a thing. Stretched out in bed, I no longer think of it thus, except artificially and by an act of will. Perhaps anything that carries me ceases to feel like a thing. Not only the bed, but also the chair, the armchair, the sofa, the stool are all forgotten, as such, when I am stretched out or seated. By dint of supporting me, bearing my weight, being under me, reliably and tacitly, they also become blurred. Occluded, unseeable. Supports – that is all they are. But also tactile presences, something other than things.

The case is not unusual. My car, when I get into

it or get out of it, is effectively a thing: a box of sheet metal with windows, placed alongside the pavement. As soon as I am driving it, however, I perceive it as an extension of my body, a mobile and alertly responsive personal bubble. The forgetting of a thing would seem to be clearly linked to the fact of our being carried, supported, borne along by it. The train is a thing while I stand on the platform looking at it. It is no longer a thing when I am travelling in it. Likewise the aeroplane, which when stationary is so oddly metallic, so mech anical, so physical. Once inside, we are simply swept along by the absolute aphrodisiac of speed.

Upright and prostrate, we inhabit different worlds. There is a lying-down universe, and there is a standing-up universe, and they have few points in common. There is likewise a sitting-down universe, an on-your-knees universe, an on-all-fours universe . . . None of them have much in common with each other. Vertical life and horizontal life cannot, by definition, be parallel lives. In bed our whole relation to space changes. And perhaps our relation to time? Do we even have the same beliefs lying down as standing up? The same emotions? The same thought-processes?

No one can be sure of answering 'yes' or 'no', unambiguously and incontrovertibly. We all have an iron conviction as to the continuity of the world and its consistency. But lie down on the ground, now, in your place of work: contemplate the ceiling; level your gaze along the ground. Is it really the *same* world you are now seeing? Whether the answer is yes or no, ask yourself one more question: in what sense yes or no? What exactly does it mean to say that this is the same world? Or that it is a different world? Stretched out, on the bed or on the ground, does what I am seeing join up with what I see standing up? And in what way? Where is the world in which these two views are reconciled? Is such a world an article of faith or an object of perception?

At the end of the day, the bed is, properly speaking, a vessel in space, rowing between both worlds.

Door

in an office, late afternoon

When I arrive, I notice dust on the door. I mean on the outside door, on the landing. Not a lot of dust, but visible enough, on the mouldings, above and at ground level. I do not know why, but I am made a little uneasy by dust on a door, especially an entrance door.

Because a door is not a thing among other things. It is double, with two visages quite distinct from, and even contrary to, each other. We tend to call any opening a 'door' or 'gate'. In a wall, a fence, a hedge, the ramparts of a city, whatever the case may be. 'Door' designates the space of free passage, the crossing point, the hiatus in the continuity of the defences. But 'door' or 'gate' is also the opposite: it is what closes the opening, seals the gap, prevents passage. Made out of wood, or bronze, or steel, or glass, the door is also what closes the doorway. A doorway is opened by a door and closed by a door. A doorway with no door would remain permanently open.

It is a thing that conjoins opposites, makes them collide, confounds them almost. We are naturally of the opinion that it must be either open or closed, there or not there. An error. The door is all of these at the same time. It unites these opposites, not as two incompatibilities but as two faces of the same reality.

The door functions like those other words that express two poles of the same reality. Words we have forgotten. *Altus*, for example, in Latin, denotes equally the height of a wall or the depth of a ditch; *sacer* denotes at once what is sacred and what is profane. We still inhabit this ambivalence: we can (in French) rejoice in a *sacré* piece of good news and then suffer from a *sacré* headache.

A presence or an absence, the door is a double thing. It protects and repulses, welcomes and turns away, is at once inside and outside. There is no spiritual itinerary that does not invoke the idea of the door. Images of doors are omnipresent in all myths and rituals, in representations of salvation and deliverance, as well as of loss. For the door unites yet separates what is on either side of it. It belongs to both sides, and in a sense to neither.

I often have the intimation, when I push open a door, that I am entering a different universe. On the other side everything will be – other. Words will no longer have the same resonances, nor gestures. That I will have to order my body and mind along new lines. In reality, this is not infrequently the case. Might this be why one should always keep a door free of dust? Because it is proper, when dealing with ambiguity, to observe the proprieties?

Sandals

at home, winter evening

I should already have put away my summer things some time ago. Perhaps I am dragging my heels out of nostalgia for the sun, for a time when I was able to go about without a pullover, even at night. To put away one's summer things is to admit that it's all over and won't come back for a long time. I start by putting sandals away in a trunk, and sandals always retain a host of memories. The canvas espadrilles that press against your big toe, and graze the top of your foot a little, which you dragged around the amphitheatres in the late afternoons when the bullfights were over. The rope-soled shoes that became as hard as wood when you walked in the warm rain with them at night and along the fringe of the waves at dawn. And the sandals full of pebbles, the sandals full of seaweed, the translucent sandals, the plastic sandals in which, long after the waves have receded and the blisters healed, are still lodged with sand and tiny pebbles, with the odd sliver of shell. Or yet again, the leather flip-flops from somewhere in the vast South, which are just held on by the big toe or the ankle, affording elementary protection against the burning sand or the furnace of the rocks.

These last are my favourites. Nothing but a single layer of leather, thick and supple, no sole to speak of, attached by a thong or a bow, at once primitive and practical. As I begin to put away the flip-flops of last summer, already worn out and grazed from walking on the rocks, I suddenly think of the contrast between this open bit of leather, as flat as my hand, and our everyday shoes. Essay topic: 'Are sandals shoes?' You have three hours.

First paragraph. The simple-minded will be inclined to judge the question as settled from the outset. In the class of things adapted for the human foot, they will say, and which are designed to protect the said foot (from wounds, cold, dirt, etc.), there is a place for moccasins as well as boots, for pumps as well as for those pointy medieval numbers. Whether open or closed, high or low, whether of leather, plastic or felt, they all belong, ultimately, in the same category.

Second paragraph (transitional; objection raised to the foregoing). The more simple-minded, observing sandals on the one hand and shoes on the other, may legitimately start to have doubts. Usually, after all, a gentleman's shoe does not let his toes show through. Nor does it expose his foot to all weathers. Perhaps the sandal is an incomplete shoe. A truncated or even embryonic shoe. A shoe consisting as much of air as of leather. A thing of holes; a virtual shoe, inferior in weight, comfort and dignity to the real thing. One of the props in the slightly embarrassing wardrobe of our summers, where everything is an abbreviation of itself (think of shorts, and of short sleeves).

Third paragraph (objections to the objection; discussion). The hopelessly simple-minded, who are capable only of observation – philosophers, in other words, if such exist – will find these conclusions surprising. After all, shoes are only solid and weatherproof in cold countries. Everywhere else, the sandal can legitimately claim parity with the shoe. Not to mention claiming precedence over the shoe, historically, throughout most of the world. Whether one thinks of that Greek statue of the victorious warrior unlacing his sandals, or whether we range further afield to India, Egypt, China – nowhere in world history does the sandal seem to have been regarded, in any respect whatsoever, as inferior.

Conclusion (radical change of tack). Nevertheless, might one not argue that the sandal is properly speaking superfluous? This must be the conclusion that the simplest of the simple-minded will reach – knowing as they do that man's feet, from time immemorial, have walked naked over earth and rocks, sand and mud, grass and moss. It is enough to take up walking barefoot again, even for a few days, to find the lightest of sandals burdensome to wear. In view of all that has been said above, one can therefore speak of this double aspect of the sandal: neither shoe nor non-shoe, it denotes the possibility of rethinking the shoe in different terms.

The little tray of exam papers is nearly full. It's time that I marked and returned them. Many significant points have been missed, and important classical references omitted (Hermes, Empedocles, etc.). Above all, few of you have grasped how the sandal offers a lesson in intermediacy, in mediation. At the interface of nature and culture, the sandal both joins and separates the foot and the ground. It embodies the frontier between worlds, the membrane that enables their coexistence. You might have mentioned, and even enlarged on, the fact that the sandal is located between flesh and earth, but also between present and past, craft and industry, East and West, North and South. And since it also contributes to movement and lightness, why not make the case for its being the hinge of the world?

Fork

Who is taking any interest in forks this morning,
other than me? An awful lot of people are surely
making use of them. Some are doubtless arranging them, or cleaning them, or restoring them.
Dealers may be busy doing business with antique
forks, museum people likewise. But who is taking
up the fork as an object of meditation, reflecting
on its form, its meaning, its place in the world and
its position (perhaps unique) in the order of things?
Who, at this moment, other than me?

I may in fact be the only person in the world, at
this precise point in time, trying to fix his attention on the essence and existence of a fork. If true,
this hypothesis only adds to my responsibility.
What if I fail? What if the sole person in the world
concentrating right now on the existence of a fork,
in what is moreover a disinterested, untrammelled

and purely idealistic spirit, finds that he has, in the end, nothing to say on the subject – would this not be a failure? Would it not be a failure for all of us, given that I am the sole representative of you all in this thankless situation? Must we therefore conclude that the whole of humanity, as embodied in my person, has, this morning, *nothing to say* about the fork?

I shall not allow the honour of *homo sapiens* to founder thus. I think I may be able to lay down the first principles for a comparative forkology. What is a fork, in effect, if not an anti-bowl? The bowl is as round and reassuring as the fork is pointed and prickly. Where the one protects, the other attacks. The first shields, the second stabs. The bowl is archaic and earthen, the fork is recent, modern, metallic. A bowl for the Ancients, a fork for the Moderns. Clearly the fork is distantly descended from the stake, the lance, the whole tribe of honed, whetted and pointed things, tempered over the fire. But to come into being, it required a different technology from that of the potter. And above all, it required a particular social evolution.

Sociologists have traced the birth and wide-spread adoption of the fork as occurring some time between the Renaissance and the Age of Reason. An end to spitting and belching. No more farting, no more fingers in the sauce. A ban even on blowing your nose into your sleeve: thus the appearance of a row of buttons on the cuff to deter one from wiping one's nose there (residually present today – look at men's jackets). Birth of the handkerchief and parallel invention of the fork. Goodbye to flesh eaten with bare hands, to hand-rolled combinations created in the palm. From now on everything proceeds by indirection, everything is mediated. Food is manipulated, kept at arm's length. The individually tailored mouthful is fixed at the end of a sharp thing. No more teeth being sunk into the roast, and bared fangs, and juices trickling down the chin; an end to the direct action of locking one's jaw and tearing off the chosen morsel. From now on, hygiene. Quality equipment. Calibration. Remote control. Abstraction. Food reduced almost to an idea of food. Ethereal mastication, pure chewing, chewing as if not chewing. Is the fork after all a platonic object? I have no notion.

In any event, the fork was born and became widely adopted at approximately the same time as scientific method and modern manners. And it may be that three aspects of the same mechanism of control are involved here. The distancing of food; the reduction of the world to mathematics;

the contractual neutralising of our relations to others. The counter-instance: peoples without forks are deprived of the exact sciences but they are spared hypocrisy. Well, more or less . . .

Finally, the fork eludes scrutiny, and to hold it is not a simple matter. I naïvely thought it was there on the kitchen table, and instead I pick it up somewhere between the Renaissance and anthropology. Perhaps it is I who am coming unstuck mentally. Is it possible that there is no such thing as a thing in isolation, sufficient unto itself? That each thing is but an element in a series, a point along a line, a moment in a temporal process?

Train Ticket

at the station,
before boarding

I am at the station, with a few minutes to spare. I have my ticket and enough time for a coffee. As I drink, I start reading the train ticket, mechanically. It is the first time I have ever tried to unravel what is printed on a ticket: name of station, number of the train, destination, time of departure and arrival, class, coach number, seat number, price, with, above and below, the injunction: 'Do not forget to punch your ticket'. Finally, various sequences of numbers of which I am, as you are, ignorant. It is reasonable to suppose that, since these numbers appear on your ticket, that somewhere, in some sort of machine, a memory has the sequence off by heart.

Now I re-examine the ticket, this time ignoring what is printed on it. A rectangle of card, the reverse side blank but scored with a brown magnetic band, the front side shaded between beige and pink. A piece of paper like any other, which can be folded, cut into pieces, burnt. All the usual physical properties. Except that this is a thing of a very particular kind. Commonplace, yet particular, because this kind of thing does not resemble, in effect, any other kind. Its sole and unique purpose is to be exchanged against another thing, or service, or benefit. It is inaccurate to say that this ticket allows me to travel: only the train – the locomotive and the carriages – actually conveys me from one place to another. It is, however, exact that I am using this ticket to travel: by witnessing to the fact that I have paid my fare, it allows me to take the train. Commercially speaking, I am a legitimate user of this train, this carriage, this seat. It is generally agreed that I exchanged money for this ticket, and I will later exchange this ticket for a journey.

Travel tickets (train, boat, plane), like innumerable tickets of every kind – underground and bus, but also cinema, theatre, museum, concert tickets – are tokens of a transaction, and they exist as things only in this function. Possession of them has no meaning except in a carefully demarcated social and physical zone. You can do nothing in

Paris with a New York subway ticket, and vice versa. These tickets are moreover generally of brief validity. They are issued for today, or for a month from today. Once they have expired, they are of no more use than any other piece of paper. You and I know all this, of course.

But have you ever felt the slightest connection between the train ticket and what you receive in exchange for it? What relation can there be between this rectangle of card and the fact that I will shortly find myself two hundred miles southwest of here? And you will have noticed, as everyone does, that there is no obvious difference in the physical appearance of tickets whose very different function is to enable me to go to London, to Berlin, or to Copenhagen. Likewise, a plane ticket to Tokyo looks rather like a plane ticket for San Francisco, or Vanuatu, or Lima. Likewise, a banknote bears no particular resemblance to any of the innumerable commodities that may be obtained in exchange for it. Every train ticket or banknote characteristically tells a double story: here is a thing that in a sense is not a thing. This thing-sign embodies a purely abstract social usage, materialised in cursory fashion by a few signs on the surface of a piece of paper.

Teapot

in a hotel, interval
between two meetings

Between two meetings, just enough time for tea. It is a long time since I drank a cup of tea, but why not? So here I am, ordering a pot of tea. But why? So many of one's actions are opaque: what one does, what one does not do, what one stops doing, what one takes up doing again. Most of our decisions, even those which strike us as taken in full awareness, and freely chosen, remain obscure and incomprehensible. So let me repeat that I have just ordered tea, and have no idea why. I used to like tea very much once upon a time, and drank it gaily, several times a day, for many years. Then one day I started drinking only coffee, without the slightest idea as to the reason for the changeover. And here I am waiting for tea to arrive, without understanding why I have ordered it. A mere craving, suddenly, just like that? It would be oddly reassuring to think so, but no, I do not think so. Manifestly, there are always reasons. And just as manifestly, I do not know what half of them are. And it is this, precisely, that one must learn to endure: to remain in ignorance of what is brewing in one's own head, without making a song and dance about it.

The waiter comes and sets down the tray. The hotel isn't much to look at, but it owns its own silver and has its standards. The teapot is muffled in a sort of quilted overcoat, supposedly to retain the heat for longer. It is slightly absurd, but well-meaning. Underneath the overcoat, white porcelain. Simple, even rustic, but very round, plump, almost podgy.

All in all, I am finding this teapot a bit perplexing. What are its characteristics? Presumably it is a descendant of the bowl, which the laws of evolution, over the course of generations, have endowed with a beak, a handle, a lid. But that answer is not satisfactory. The bowl structure can be found in many things other than teapots. The teapot must have other defining qualities. But which? No doubt its particularity resides in its function. Which is to be upstream from the cup, so to speak, in the pecking order of functions between kettle and lips. There are things whose destinies are routinely linked by the mere sequentiality of our human actions, although they have no intrinsic connection to each other. The teapot is a sort of village-chief bowl, an officer-class bowl, a special operations bowl: infusion, maceration, diffusion of tea-leaf aromas in boiling water. The strange labour of the teapot: an activity without noise, without activity, wholly vested in time, heat and confinement. A hidden process of ripening. The earth, the womb, the brain – all of these spheres of production refuse to be rushed, and do their work in the dark, in secrecy. The teapot belongs to this family.

It is also a thing which bears the traces of its use, accumulates minute deposits, the patina of age. Related to the pipe, to earthenware plates, to unpolished terracotta floors, to things that let themselves be written upon by time, with a fine, brownish film. In effect, such things do not assume a form as such, once and for all. They are always in a state of becoming. They wear but do not wear out. On the contrary, they put on weight, they thicken. In the course of time, they become more rounded and the light plays off them differently. They are never finished, becoming at once more and more smoothly accomodating and more and more densely themselves.

Computer

winter night, at home

Luminous, giving out a uniform light. Before being a thing of plastic, cables, processor, keyboard and accessories, the computer is above all light. Constant, uninterrupted light. Indifferent to what it transmits, unalterable. Whatever the text, the images, the figures, the music, the film, the numbers, the accounts, the distractions, the work in progress, the research, the messages from friends, the news, the rough drafts, the completed texts, the discoveries, the mistakes, the sudden freezes, the dead ends, the procedures, the breakdowns . . . Before all of this, the computer is light. Impassive and unearthly light. Inseparable from all of its functions and facilities, indissolubly part of the screen, as much as text or image, and yet impossible really to confuse with either.

Turning on my computer this evening, I sense

how close is the affinity this light creates between computer and consciousness. Without its luminous halo, we would have a very different relationship to this machine. But the pearl nimbus, moonlike, persistent, tenacious, and at the same time so supremely neutral, makes this object difficult to classify. It is like some clone of – or something that clones – consciousness itself. Because of its constant state of pulsating awareness, we tend unconsciously to think of the computer as an extension of our mental life.

A sort of proxy brain. An annex, an extension. Each time it turns itself on, I have the physical sensation of setting in motion some part of my mind. There are ideas, sentences, even entire books contained inside it, which could only have come into being, as far as I am concerned, in this form. Open or closed, on or off, connected or disconnected, light or dark, access given or access denied – what it comes down to, every time, is an extension or contraction of my field of consciousness.

This curious object, half-thing and half-self, is a product of my generation: of all of us who are intermediate and ambivalent in respect of its operations. The generation which followed is more at home with it, handles it more intuitively, uses it more imaginatively and freshly than we who had to learn it as adults, rather than imbibe it as infants. Nonetheless, it is my generation that maintains a magical relationship with the computer-thing. For we originally learnt to read and write quite differently. Books, exercise books, inkwells, crossings out, blots (the name for large ink stains made on exercise books in schools, once upon a time – younger readers please note). Much later, when we grew up, we had to undergo a metamorphosis, a migration from paper to keyboard, from pen to screen, without any idea, moreover, of where exactly this was leading us.

In the history of my own relationship to this thing, by now already a long story, I used at first to write out rough drafts on paper. I would use the luminous box only for making a fair copy, like a superior typewriter, to achieve a result with no crossings out. Then one day I made the leap. A few scribbled notes on a piece of paper, as a security blanket; then fingers on the keyboard, eyes on the screen, forever after. Hours, weeks, months, years: articles, conferences, essays, books – just like that, by direct method. I can now barely remember how to write by hand, except to scrawl the odd word, a quick note, a phone number in a hurry. Writing, henceforth, is on a screen. Otherwise, there seems a lack of space, a lack of fluency, of clarity, of control – the absence of calibration, of typefaces, of justified margins, of formatting. I am not convinced that the writing itself has been affected, for good or ill. Faster, perhaps. Cleaner, certainly. But no other side-effects. Then one day, without really knowing why, I suddenly started writing in longhand once more. Since that time, I have written some works on a screen, others by hand. I let it happen of its own accord. It is the texts themselves that decide.

People of my generation have one foot in the virtual world, the other in the world of ink and the noise of scratching paper. Between the old order – books, papers, shelves, rotary presses, newspapers, kiosks – and the new: screens, servers, sites, immediacy, mobility, the instant purveyance of pure information. Between these worlds there stretches an infinitely receding corridor of doors and trapdoors: scanners, numerical encodings, character recognition. The old order was fed piecemeal through this multitude of doors, into this new thing without a name, fluid and global, where texts are no longer separate from one another, but form a single vast tablecloth.

This infinite cloud of language has its dramas. It is shaken by tempests, crossed by submarine storms and systemic faults. It has its own version of tectonic plates, of continental drift, of species evolution. The computer of yesteryear, an archaic, autistic box, is today an open window on to the multicultural swamp. Where life is omnipresent. Proof: the virus, whose existence brings the world of computers closer to reality – unclean, unhealthy, hobbled, mutant reality. And – against a background of incessant computing activity that eludes consciousness – this uniform, unwavering light.

Sponge

bathroom, morning

Among the things of uncertain status, the half-alive things, let us not forget the sponge. I am struck by the force of this while cleaning the sink. Things that absorb other things are rare. Among them, the sponge possesses the faculty, seemingly inexhaustible, of absorbing and giving back. It swallows the traces, the grime, the marks, and makes them disappear. It eliminates so as to start over again. In this way it offers a different model of memory from the computer. The latter retains every particular, point by point, binomially, transforming all information into a sequence of ones and zeros. The sponge has an entirely different way of remembering. It impregnates itself with information, ingests it through every pore, swells up. It retains liquids as does the bowl, yet in an entirely dissimilar fashion. For it takes them into its very self, into its sponge-substance. It swallows and absorbs everything into its memory, its fibrous heart, even to the point of choking and changing colour, even if this means having to squeeze it all out again. It memorises by retention. The sponge conserves in its folds far more than one thinks. We too go through existence like sponges. Like computers too, perhaps, encoding and decoding, but also categorically like sponges, storing in our fibres the pith and the dross of so many places, emotions, bodies, objects, smells and instants of time that it is impossible to preserve them all indefinitely. Impossible also to reconstruct them all. Or even distinguish them all with any clarity. A porous thing, in constant circulation, passing over different surfaces. Soaking it all up.

Freezer

end of day, kitchen

I run a sponge over the freezer. Some sauce has
spilled over it, leaving a brown smear on the white
enamel. A squirt of colour on the impassive surface. It will be absorbed promptly, and the smooth,
white coldness restored to itself. The passage of
a sponge. All is as before, as if nothing had happened. The north face of the freezer will glitter
once more: vertical, mineral, snow-clad.

The freezer is a machine of secrets. It belongs
to the family of thing-enigmas, which perplex us
and which we approach with hesitation: the sense
of a surface, of volume, of a door, of an interior
which can be accessed. All of which tells us next to
nothing. Things of this kind are self-enclosed,
keeping their counsel. Boxes containing mysteries.
We become used to them, we draw our own conclusions, but we never really discover how they

work. How exactly is the cold generated? How does it manage to remain constant? Why is it so intense? Why does intense cold preserve, for days and weeks and months, foodstuffs that otherwise decompose and rot? We are used to all of this. It no longer astonishes us. In fact, we do not understand the first thing about it. Most of us, at least. I am aware that there are engineers and biologists out there, individuals who understand the why and the wherefore, and who are capable of explaining. But they are exceedingly few, and they tend perforce to be restricted to their expertise. Thus, someone who understands the functioning of a freezer may well be stumped when it comes to explaining a television set, or a computer, or a boiler.

It is the way with these boxes, that he who possesses the secrets of one is ignorant about those of another. Ignorance becomes the thing we all have in common, and increases inexorably in step with scientific and technological development. The proliferation of efficient and complex machines, highly sophisticated and eminently logical, leads also to the proliferation of stupefied and passive states of mind. Confronted by these closed things, endowed with powers that are explicable only by others, we revert to an essentially infantile state of mind.

We do not like to acknowledge this. It is not agreeable to see ourselves ignorant, passive, no longer able to penetrate the world of appearances. Reduced to folk wisdom. Barely capable of putting together, from scraps of knowledge or experience, some provisional descriptions to fill in the gaps. A thousand little myths concocted in the dark, like so many obscure fetishes of explanation. Somewhere between laughter and fear.

In the case of the freezer, at first you are filled with wonderment. Henceforth at home there will be a permanent availability of fresh fish and meat, vegetables and fruits, intact and edible. What could be more empowering? Yes, empowering: what a victory over time, over decay, over death. And this machine for the suspension of time and its deleterious effects, not only does it conserve the basic perishables, it even preserves your own lovingly prepared concoctions. It is beyond the bounds of reason, and admittedly it has engendered more than a few monsters: cubes of soup, blocks of sauce, unbreakable juices, mincemeat stones. The metamorphosis of liquid into solid, of softness into stiffness. Garden peas turned pebbles, fish transformed to logs. A form of alchemy? A machine for transubstantiation?

I am suddenly reminded of the Himalayas, the

foothills, the state of Sikkim. Where I learnt – from seeing murals of them depicted on the portals of a lamasery – that Buddhists believe in the existence of cold hells. Ours are always full of braziers and the smoke of furnaces. We all go up in flames. Tibetan Buddhists have their hells of fire, much like ours, but also their hells of ice, where bodies turn blue and stiffen, petrify, congeal. The freezer is of this family.

Beneath its white door and its enamelled calm, there stretches a misty underworld, at the confines of death, where life is suspended and time immobilised by cold. Which raises a cat's cradle of questions: is it heat that kills everything? Does cold arrest time itself? And how? What is the relation between life, temperature and death? What exactly is alive about frozen embryos? Or frozen sperm? What is the nature of this sealed-off zone, created by frost, neither wholly dead nor completely alive? In what stratum of being is this infra-existence of protracted duration maintained? Is the freezer really a sort of anti-clock, which traffics with death?

Mobile Phone

on a staircase,
between two meetings

Just as I start to descend the staircase, it rings in my pocket. It always rings just as I start to . . . The mobile phone, universally worshipped and spared no expense. It lets me speak to anyone, anywhere. In spite of which, it belongs firmly in the category of worst things. And in the category of the two-faced: both help and hindrance. Its convenience, its proximity and its ubiquity are also what make it intolerable.

Here we have a thing that emits incongruous tunes, or vibrates, or flashes, just to let you know, inside your pocket, or strapped to your belt, or in your car, or even in close proximity to your heart, that there are people who want to speak to you, urgently, this instant, to get information out of you, to offer you work, to make plans, to give you their news. And who want to speak to you here and now, in person, wherever you are, whatever you might be doing.

The mobile phone is like the watch: it ruthlessly submits you to external constraints. But there is something depersonalised and imperturbably regular about the watch, whereas the mobile phone is galvanised by the whims of individuals, and makes you likewise dependent, in random fashion, on their needs and caprices. The result is the sudden and arbitrary intervention in your daily life of the peculiarities of others, brusquely interfering with your activities, your thoughts, your haunts, which have mostly nothing to do with them, and which find them more or less intolerable.

You will say that it is the same with the traditional telephone: without warning, sudden invasion by absolutely anyone, a very advanced form of brutality in human relations. And, built into the very rationale of the telephone, complete unconcern as to what a single moment in the life of a thinking being is capable of meaning, and what the ringing of a telephone may disturb or destroy. But with traditional phones, in spite of everything, you could always leave the room. It was possible to escape momentarily from this archaic receiver, tethered to its post. You could arrange things for a while so as to slip away from all possibility of being contact-ed, got in touch with, waylaid. But the mobile does everything in its power to prevent such abscondings.

You know as well as I do that it does not succeed. There is a whole range of tricks that enable one to outflank this permanent invasion of unwanted voices wherever one goes. The voice mail, the text message, the call-return and other such tactics allow you to put off and postpone. Nonetheless, you are supposed to pick up and return your messages as soon as possible, throw yourself upon them breath-less with attention, and just a touch of guilt, as soon as you are back online. Since the basic principle, the entire rationale and avowed ambition of the portable phone is perpetual connection, non-stop, limitless, lifelong, night and day. Along with accom-modating your faxes, your photos, news items, preferences, emails, voice messages, text messages, television channels, favourite films, health tips, pulse rate, blood pressure, glucose levels and – if there's room – accident and emergency numbers in case of danger, even minus battery, not to mention (why not?) FM radio plus the weather forecasts and the stock exchange results. Everything necessary for survival. All this and only one commandment: Thou Shalt Not Disconnect.

The object: to engineer a new inside and outside. In other times, people inhabited one world, out there. Now, however, there are two worlds; and those not inside the brave new world are out there in the cold, disconnected. They do not know what they are missing. Perhaps they are already lost, like those tribes belonging to an earlier stage of humanity which are said to linger on into the present, in certain coastal or mountainous regions still without network coverage. This outside dwindles by the day. Coverage is wellnigh universal. Portable phones get more and more portable. The more they shrink, the more functions they are able to master. Things for communication, machines of solitude. Be In When You Are Out. Be Free, Everywhere and Always – courtesy of the smallest and most commonplace little servo-control mechanism.

Questions II

As the experiment progresses, I am aware that it raises more questions than I would have thought possible. So I shall try once more to take my bearings, though I am conscious that these are becoming less and less steady.

In fact, I am no longer certain where any particular thing begins and ends. The frontier is not marked. It is as if we overlap with things and aspects of things are buried inside us. This is no doubt a recent phenomenon. Obviously, there has always been interaction, for example with those things to which memories are attached – objects belonging to one's father, or one's beloved. Or there is the case of presents, which preserve the trace of the giver, or things brought back from travels: pebbles from hiking trips, trinkets from faraway places. People and places have always been implicated with things. But that was a matter of individual psychology, the association of ideas, the mechanisms of memory. No one ever actually confused people with things.

Between them and us there was, after all, a radical disjunction. Persons were endowed with reason, consciousness, free will and language. Things had none of these. Persons consequently had rights and duties, and merited respect. Things had none of this. Think of Kant, or Roman law, and the libraries devoted to this question. Today, on the other hand, everything is a lot less clear. Between persons and things confusions are brewing. Between those things surrounding the person we love and that person in himself or herself, we no longer perceive a radical difference. Fetishism has become the story of everyday life. It also happens, more and more frequently, that a so-called person represents a thing as far as a second thing is concerned. For example, as far as an ATM machine is concerned, a consumer is nothing more than a credit card; as far as a decoder is concerned, a TV viewer means a remote control, and so on.

A few steps further and we shall be giving the world of objects the right to vote; things will be able to inherit, assert copyright over images of themselves, demand *habeas corpus* and the presence of a lawyer in the event of police custody. Are these changes – the transformation of things into persons, already well advanced – obscurely and obversely related to the transformation of people into things: the history of deportations and mass murders, the multiplication of prostheses and implants, the inevitable cloning of everything, which is by now generalised, commonplace and accelerating by the day? No, for this would of course be to take too simple a view of the matter. Everything is probably implicated in a far more wily and unpredictable manner than a simple symmetrical opposition would suggest. But what is clear is that the border-crossing between things and people gets busier and busier.

What interests me, more than the border, is the fold. I would like to discover how things are folded up, what ancient meanings are sometimes concealed in the folds that constitute a thing. With each thing, ideally we should be able to unwrap what it contains of compacted words, erased words, for the most part barely construable. How to go about this? Does the object-world have a tip or edge, to take hold of which would be the right place to begin? Or does the object-world offer us no leverage? Or again, without our knowing if this is better or worse, might the world of things have any number of starting points? May it not be taken hold of everywhere, beginning with the first thing that comes to hand, at random, indifferently? After all, no particular thing is any more of a thing than any other thing. Or any less. Whichever you start with will do. Whoever wants to know about things can address no matter which of them for illumination. The toothbrush is on a par with the sofa, and the bottle-opener with the computer. Although the general features which they share may be self-evidently few. The case is otherwise when it comes to unpicking an individual thing, one thing in partic-ular, a thing unlike any other. It is here that we may hope, with a little luck, to get caught up in the folds.

Perhaps we must resign ourselves to an absence of method. And perhaps it would be presumptu-ous, and illusory, to want to establish a method. Naturally it is somewhat disorientating to embark on an experiment with no guidelines whatever, and seemingly without protocols. An experiment so lacking in scientific spirit: random observa-tions, uncertain rules, improbable results. As if one decided to mount an expedition to some *terra incognita*, without knowing where it was situated or what one expected to find there. And to set off immediately, moreover, without any idea of what provisions to take.

*

Such a procedure is not without its risks. I think of it as a game in the first instance, a distraction, whose purpose is merely to see what will happen. Hang on, I say to myself, this is interesting, let's have a go, why not? Or at least, I choose to believe that this is what I think. And having embarked, I become aware that it is all a bit less simple, perhaps less innocent. After all, to become a thing is to render oneself non-human, to exit from life. Clearly, we are all destined to do this, to become corpse-things – but what kind of risk am I taking if I try to approach this condition from the inside, so to speak, just to see what it is like?

I realise that it is impossible to penetrate this enigma, the veil of things, which no human life can resolve. But one might at least restate it, walk around it on various sides, cast some light on its outer confines. To do so is to take one step along a road without end. And it may mean having to spy on things for hours and days on end, sometimes in vain, sometimes with meagre results. In this peculiar chase, we do not know what the prey looks like exactly, nor how to trap it. Nor even when the hunt is over. We have no idea what the truth might actually look like. We try to capture it in spite of everything. We never know, ultimately, to what degree we are in possession of it, nor if what we are clasping triumphantly is merely an illusion that will evaporate tomorrow.

These disappointments do not prevent the chase from being headlong. For a mere rumour of the truth, uncertain and ephemeral, a whole lifetime is not too high a price to pay. Which is unreasonable, clearly. Individuals who think of themselves as philosophers have in common the desire for a knowledge which is constantly receding, or in hiding. They are ready to give everything for a glimpse of the infinite. Without knowing if it is illusory or not. Nor does this stop them in their tracks. They are bent to their task by something experienced momentarily. Possibly there can be no philosophy without an experience of this kind. There are celebrated and moving examples: Augustine called by the voice of a passing child, Descartes shaken by a dream about a new science, Pascal's night of tears, Rousseau beneath the tree in Vincennes, Valéry cast adrift into abstract thought on the tide of the small hours. There are modest, casual versions of this in everyone's experience. Some of these nights of the soul give rise to definitive contributions. Others – for the most part – lead only to outlines and beginnings.

What importance, after all, attaches to the type of the experiment or the quality of the results? All that counts is its faithfulness. And accuracy, at least for once in a lifetime. A common expression, but it has been clear to me since I first pondered the question 'How are things?' that I would have to make the voyage among things at least once in my life. Which means entering the *terra incognita* where they are set down. A region beyond language, beyond thought as such, beyond true and false. This land of things, inert, inanimate, incapable of feeling, of reproducing themselves, or of healing themselves, is an immense region. A relatively small number of living organisms move amongst countless multitudes of lifeless objects, and no one pays any attention to this state of affairs. It ought to be cause for constant astonishment. Which is not really the case.

How does it happen that our things do not inhabit the same world as ourselves? Even the simplest, most reassuring things are at bottom inhuman, impossible to speak of. These everyday and intimate things are entirely other, without our knowing anything of their otherness. My body moves among things, is surrounded by them, makes use of them, thinks it knows them. Despite which, there remains between us an unbridgeable abyss. I am able to see, touch, taste, breathe and listen; I am activated by time, by memory and desire, hopes and recollections; I experience fatigue or pleasure, joy or sadness. Things have none of these things. They remain outside of time, and neither feel nor experience anything. Deprived of consciousness. Without sense, without motion. Dead. No, not even dead. For ever and always to one side of life.

This world so different to ours seems to be an absolute enigma. Especially as there are so many imponderables. In what sense and to what extent is there a life of things? To what degree are we, too, things? Capable of becoming things? Death, once again, is the ineluctable thing-state of the human body. But otherwise, in other directions, how many ways are there of leaving oneself behind, or of attempting to do so? How many routes lead out of the world of words, or attempt to do so? How many ways are there to negotiate the frontier – which we sense to be at once porous and impassable – between us and things? And with what possible side-effects?

I have no idea. I hope to have more of an idea. I will therefore press on. But not without fears. It has occurred to me more than once, over these past weeks, that this game is perhaps dangerous.

To edge closer to the world of things is to strike out in the direction of silence, the out-of-self, the inorganic, the non-human. Perhaps one may feel the joy of giving oneself the slip. Or perhaps one might encounter instead, on the way or right at the end, something unforeseen.

PANIC

In front of me there are things: there they are, hard, distinct, weighty. They have their space, where they combine and add to their numbers; and their time, when they form new links in their chain, fan out, survive each other. I am buried under their presence, suffocated inside their space, carried along inside their time. I was born amongst them and will die amongst them, while their thingy reality and their muteness live on.

Here, it would seem, is what binds me to this world.

But what exactly are these things?

Jean-Toussaint Desanti,
'Notebook of 1945', in
Of servitude and freedom
(unpublished)

Rubber Boots

seaside, winter morning

It happens slowly, insidiously. I cannot tell the precise moment. Perhaps when the days begin to grow longer. I think of the proverb: 'The days of the Three Kings [that is, from Epiphany onwards] are drawn out with a silken thread.' Is this slow thread of light making me ill? I start to see things in terms more or less viscous. Everything seems to weigh more, to grow heavy, to slump. As I said, this does not happen all at once. Pictures, places, objects remain familiar. Their dazzling normality reassures me. I know that they at least are not affected. Their colours are unchanged, their edges perfectly defined. Some kind of serene obstinacy animates them, so to speak, and allows them visibly to resist infection. Initially, at least. Then that too starts to change. They begin by getting just a little drab. Then their edges begin to lose clarity.

Their surfaces seem to become puffy, at first imperceptibly, then more and more obviously. Finally everything sinks and sags, leaving a sense of disquiet and desolation.

I decide to take a few days off. Perhaps the feeling will come to a halt by the seaside. I adore the sea in winter, because it remains, as far as possible, unchanged. The cold and the light are those of winter, but the sea, the water itself, bears no trace of difference. The countryside contracts, shrivels up, loses its leaves, hardens, becomes a shaven penitent. The mountains give themselves over to a white silence; the city draws in its skirts, and capitulates to greyness. The sea, on the contrary, even in mist, even in a louring wind, keeps its immutable reserve. You may have doubts as to whether this is entirely accurate. No matter. The idea suits me. It confirms my winter walks along the beaches.

I get out my rubber boots, clean them up, put my hand right down inside to check that there are no mice. Where did this habit come from? What mouse would dream of taking refuge in this wobbling cavern, reeking of rubber? Nothing further removed from sandals than these long closed tubes. The foot is entirely imprisoned inside them. Every time you put them on you have to punch through that moment when the exercise seems doomed to failure, the foot stuck, the rubbery bend impossible to negotiate. Finally, with enough persistence it gives way, unblocks suddenly and your heel strikes the bottom.

Every time, an odd feeling of suppleness at first, as if you are not wearing shoes but only a second, thicker skin, a mobile protection. The fleetness of the huntress, the combat-readiness of khaki, combined with the calm which comes of wading about in muddy pools and marine ebbtide. In the event, things start off well but always turn out badly. Rubber does not protect against the cold, and it converts perspiration into trapped moisture, compounding the cold penetrating from outside with a glacial sweatiness on the inside. Your skin no longer feels protected but imprisoned, suffocated, waterlogged; the boots, in a few kilometres or a few hours, become sarcophagi; they eat your flesh, putrefy it almost, leaving it pickled, swollen, deathly pale. It's not a question of different types of rubber boot, of replacing bad quality with good quality. It is a matter of fate. Not even individual fate. Collective fate: whatever protects also imprisons, whatever comforts becomes murderous. The light step turns to stone, the ramble becomes a sepulchre.

The waves alone remain. Time to go home.

Washing Machine

laundry room, end of day

Walking by the sea changes nothing. On the contrary, it makes things worse. I have the impression that my own flesh is turning to water. Starting with my feet. In cold rubber boots, then sweaty rubber boots, my feet themselves will end by crumbling, as prelude to a general dissolution. I amuse myself grimly by reflecting that beside the sea the evidence would be briskly dispersed, remote as the experience might prove from any Freudian feeling of the oceanic.

I get back to the old, weather-beaten house, light a wood fire and begin, blindly and creaturely, as other humans do in temperate climates when they are chilled to the bone, by holding up the soles of my feet and palms of my hands to the flames. The rubber boots have stayed in the store-room, and I have removed the marshy socks, with a mental note to remember to put them into the washing machine in a moment. There is, fortunately, a washing machine.

Waiting for my blood to circulate, I idly conjure up, in my chimney corner, a prehistoric scenario. When did we first begin washing clothes? Probably not for as long as clothes have existed. There was a time (who knows?) when we wore animal skins until they rotted, or vegetable skins – creepers, dried leaves – that were unwashable. Besides, travellers of a few generations back have described (or invented) how Huns and Tartars living on horseback would let their clothes decompose, from wear and tear and filth, without ever cleaning them or even removing them.

Nonetheless, the habit of washing took hold quite some time ago. As women's work, the world over. Rivers, streams, wash houses. Whether in the dampness of the tropics or against the sharp north wind, whether standing or sitting or crouching, for century after century women have soaked, scrubbed, rinsed and dried the washing. Countless entire lifetimes, passed in the company of threads and fibres. Washing the clothes of mothers, of husbands, of brothers, of warriors, of children. Sewing and stitching and darning too, but first and foremost washing, drying, folding. Upkeep and repetition. A cyclical affair, like cooking and cleaning. Or like life itself.

Then relatively recently, to cut a long story short, a machine takes over the job. Not that this machine escapes the rule of the cycle: drum, cylinder, rotation. In sequence. Wash, Rinse, Spin. In between, a bit of technical bluff: dials, programmes, controls, tables for different materials and degrees of water hardness. So much powder in your eyes. The heart of the matter remains cyclical and rotary. For longer than we can think back, washing goes around and around. Impurity, ablution, purity. And eternal return. Like souls, evidently.

The washing machine is thus a thing of the cosmic variety. You stuff dead souls into it. Everything turns around. The water effaces the past, the stain, the memory. Deluge after deluge, it penetrates the most recalcitrant fibres, dissolves the most intimate blemishes, cleans away former lives. From one cycle to the next, the new emerges from the old. And when everything that was formerly the case seems definitively soaked away, the door opens, the porthole releases the cleansed souls, soon to be dried out, ready for a new life. Naturally, they can recall nothing. Just like new, ready to go and sin once more.

Perhaps the washing machine is a last survivor

of the mystery cults? Initiation, death, rebirth – cosmic matters, which always feature ablutions, cleansings, immersions, rotations, cycles. This must be what is meant today by the cult of the domestic goddess.

Tombstone

country cemetery,
on a featureless Sunday

To refresh my thoughts, I go for a walk in the village cemetery. I know it well, have frequented it for years. The small group of families, pressed together like sardines on either side of the little paths; the porcelain flowers discolouring from year to year. On many of the tombs, a brown and green moss covers the names. Within a few yards of each other, different centuries coexist, as indicated by the different written forms of the alphabet, different kinds of cross, or by the variety of cast-iron enclosures all eaten away with rust.

I feel a certain fondness for this bric-à-brac of conventions, this assortment of bare props that strive to hold on to memory, keep the trace of a name, a date, sometimes even a face. Medallions with photographs of soldiers, sailors. Books rigidly open at a set page, their only text 'Eternal Regrets', or 'In Memory of Uncle'. The nephew in question is no doubt resting in the next aisle. The eternal regrets have in turn perished, and the man who felt such emotions is gently decomposing in a nearby cemetery. All that remain are the tombstone and the funerary trimmings.

Can the tomb be described as a thing? Yes, clearly. A block of granite with pediment, side aisles and a bowl in front for flowers. A smooth block, polished or grained. Depending on the century, and above all on the wealth of the deceased. A solid object, bounded, densely compacted, intended to resist time. Equally clearly, however, the tombstone is less of a thing than a sign. It discharges a sacred function: as a marker, a memory trace, a gap, a marked-off void, a point of passage.

Together with the bowl, the tomb is the earliest human thing. Fashioned as a thing, but filled entirely with beliefs, histories, myths. A thing closed to the living, open upon an elsewhere. An absence. A silence, as of mute refusal. A thing par excellence, then? Possibly. The headstone at once hides and designates the corpse. In this sense, it is supremely a thing, one face of which is flat and level, the other invisible. One full, the other hollow, empty. Humans began by defining themselves thus. The tomb distinguishes human time from featureless, animal eternity. The dead lie in a circumscribed place, the corpse seated or reclining, surrounded by familiar objects, accompanied by ritual traces and constraints – by such signs do we recognise our own. We know, even without the words, that this ensemble indicates us, that it signals to us. Everyone knows, and each of us forgets.

Standing at the highest point of the cemetery, on a slight overhang, among the watering cans and the compost, I wonder whether we should not reverse our sense of this entirely, and tell ourselves that things, and things alone, retain memory, preserving names and dates, doing memory work, obdurately, lastingly, while it is we who are amnesiac and transient. A step further. Perhaps we should acknowledge that every thing has direct access to death, another dimension, an underside, facing backwards, like a breath on the nape of the neck. Perhaps we should be telling ourselves that things alone have virtues, ideas, that they alone observe the proprieties. That we do no more than follow behind, as best we can, which is not a great deal. That each thing is an intermediary between appearance and nothingness, between presence and what is inaccessible. Sometimes we have intimations of this, but most of the time we fail.

Or indulge ourselves in daydreams. Meanwhile the metal gate creaks, and an old lady enters with her cane, some flowers in her hand. The gravel crunches. The sounds chase away whatever it is that we should be telling ourselves and acknowledging. Too many flights of fancy and over-excitement. Under this thing in a cemetery there are merely other things. Beneath the headstone, a coffin, bones. Nothing more. Nothing to worry about. Nothing interesting, even. Things beneath things. The sky is getting overcast.

Hand Drill

in the shed, public holiday

Doing odd jobs, in the house by the sea, I am reminded of my abiding partiality for screws. I like their determination. They do not deviate from their objective, but sink straight in. Not all at once, however, not in a straight line, thick-headedly, as nails do. They proceed rather by indirections, turning and pivoting around themselves, making every use of their grooves. And when you have turned their heads sufficiently, they come to a stop, buried to the hilt in the material in question, holding together whatever you wish to assemble.

They do not always manage to bite unassisted into the material – too hard, too smooth – they are being asked to penetrate. But the drill is on hand to prepare the ground, boring a preliminary hole at the required spot. This tool could not be simpler,

– 147 –

or craftier. No electrical device has yet provided a satisfactory alternative. For the action of a drill must be slow and searching. It must know when to stop – to the nearest millimetre. The bit of an electric drill is too eager and reckless, so to speak. Besides, it drills in a cylindrical fashion, whereas the hand drill orbits around a point, in conical fashion, like a screw. In fact, the hand drill as such is no more than a hand screw, a two-way screw, equally capable of burying itself and of withdrawing, acting simply as a harbinger.

Those who really know what they are doing rest the handle in the hollow of their palm, applying a regular pressure, depending on the resistance of the material. There are several pitfalls to avoid. Acting too harshly and damaging the wall or surface. Drilling too far and leaving a gaping hole, far too wide for the purpose. Or finding yourself stuck, and unable to reverse out. A few small pleasures, on the other hand, are to be relished: the muted cry of the drill in the course of penetration, the increasing heat of the shaft, the final outpouring of sawdust from the sides of the hole.

We can rely on students of such things to provide an exact and judicious account of the sexual displays of the drill. Of more interest, perhaps, to emphasise the differences. What separates the process from coital behaviour: the spiralling, Archimedean aspect, perhaps, or the irreversible nature of the action. If anything, it puts one more in mind of mental operations. It evokes the way an idea spirals its way through the mind, leaving a permanent trace. As if a thought were boring its way through flesh. Which seems indeed to be confirmed by experts in neurophysiology and connoisseurs in the business of torture, each of whom is, after his fashion, an odd-job man.

Perhaps, to become free, one must succeed in drilling one's head outwards from inside. Providing one has ideas that are sufficiently spiralling and conical. It takes a little time to pierce the cranium, naturally. But once the hole is drilled, the air can circulate. Something that mystics know all about.

Bottle Opener

in the kitchen, one evening

Coming back to town on this occasion has not had the usual shock effect. In fact, I am still floating. A curious condition. You could say that, to make successful contact with things, you have to step outside of yourself. But for the moment I have touched down nowhere in particular. I am suspended, without moorings. A plane in slow motion, before starting its descent.

Which does not prevent one from being thirsty. Why am I so thirsty this evening? Oh yes, the anchovies. I need something carbonated, with bubbles. There must be some fizzy water or soda in the fridge. Yes. Magnificent and chilled, a large bottle full of bubbles. And at the top, metallic and crimped, the cap. Silver-patterned, after a fashion. And entirely resistant to fingers and thumbs. Clamped to the neck of the bottle with all of its many claws, unconditionally attached. What I need is a bottle opener.

I cannot lay hands on it at first. It is hiding in a drawer full of kitchen things – can openers, apple corers, corkscrews, various knives – underneath them all, completely flat. As I take hold of it, the idea crosses my mind that this primitive tool (a scooped-out head, a lever) bears witness to or mimes an ancient ritual.

Red plastic for a body. Brushed aluminium for a head. Nothing but a bottle opener. A contraption of no consequence, indispensable only in very specific circumstances. Well suited to its function. Effective, in its way: insert cap at an angle, apply leverage, observe an instant hissing of the contents, and ejection of the bent bottle-top, complete with metallic noise. Entirely banal, without interest, purely functional. Except that, as I open the bottle, I have glimpsed something quite different. A head locked in a vice, an upward pressure, a cracking of vertebrae, then the head falling beside the body, rolling at its feet. Opening a bottle, pulling off a head. A decapitation – or, rather, an opening up of the skull, a lifting of the roof. A getting rid of the cover that prevents the circulation of energy.

Might this be so? That in order to glimpse

another reality we have to take the roof off our head? Stories of mystics and poets crowd in. The dream of seeing without a head. I am thinking of Georges Bataille, or of the cover that André Masson designed for the magazine *Acéphale* ['Headless']. The age-old fantasy: finally to rid oneself of the encumbrance of a head, escape once and for all from logic, from words in their proper places. Quick! And let it all roll far away! Let us rediscover the life of sensations running beneath our conscious mental life, whether in its lunar or solar aspect. And learn the animal potential for divinity. Or else, suddenly awakened, let us follow the most extreme ascetics of India, let us go and bury ourselves upright, with only our heads protruding above ground, and just as suddenly severed. A thing at last among things. A pure thought-bubble, in its burst condition, without name or form.

The desire for oblivion runs deep. It rubs up against me slowly, from time to time. Its existence is universally acknowledged, after all. Always masked, yet perfectly visible. It lies in waiting, and works its effects in silence. Despite which, I have long considered it the worst of delusions, the false path. Life is not a matter of becoming a thing, nor of going over to the side of things. Rather, if this has any meaning, it is a question of uncorking whatever is blocking the world for us, as one opens a bottle. I am grateful to my thirst . . .

Answering Machine

'Hi, it's Isabelle . . . Well, I was just wondering how you are. Hope all's well. See you soon! Call me!' – 'Daddy it's Marie I need to know if it's OK for me to go to the [something something] concert of [inaudible] on Saturday and can you pay for me if so it's £20 big kiss.' – 'Good afternoon, this is the reception at Doctor Decker's surgery. Would you please confirm the appointment for Tuesday next at 5.30 p.m.?' – 'Paul here, got your message, that's fine, flat 6, bottom buzzer, see you in a bit.'

The voices are all different, and so is the delivery. Vocabulary, phrasing, pronunciation, different in every case. And yet these different voices are identically contained inside a box. Packed tightly into this cube of black plastic, with dial and buttons. They are captives somewhere inside, but there is no means of knowing where or how. The mystery of voice machines. We no longer pay them the slightest attention, out of habit. Nonetheless, it's a weird business.

I have just bought the newspaper, some bread, some tomatoes. I could now just as well go to a meeting, or go and listen to a debate, or go to sleep or hop on a bus or do some work. Whatever I do, people will arrive in the black box. No, not people. Voices, merely voices, detached, disembodied, without faces or expressions. Suspended voices, without any interlocutor, all of them recognisable and yet also distorted, not by the recording so much as by the situation. These voices sound altered, estranged, by the absence of another voice, and yet despite this they reserve a space for the other. They project themselves into the void, towards the possibility of the other, towards the idea of his or her imminent return. They address the future tense of his deferred hearing of their words. But they are speaking not merely from another place, the next street or the next hemisphere, but from another moment in time. They call from one time to another time. It is their destiny to sojourn in a time out of joint, deferred and distant.

For my part, I can never hear them as though I were present. True enough, I have returned home.

I listen to my messages, as you can see. At the same time, just as I hear in these voices their absence, I also sense, in the act of listening, my earlier absence. When they speak to me, I am not there. When I am there, listening to them, I persist in not being entirely there, by the very fact that listening to them refers me back to my own absence.

The answering machine is a thing constructed entirely out of absence. In spite of its name, no one ever answers anyone by its means. Between the message left on one machine to the message left on another, it often happens that we carry on the semblance of dialogue. But these are phantom conversations, conducted between telephones, voice boxes, recording machines, things that capture sound and sense and time. All of it infinitely replayable. Rabelais invented the existence of frozen words, preserved by the cold, which became newly audible when the ice thawed. We have gone one better by managing, without changing anything on the surface, to freeze time itself, at its heart's core.

Supermarket Trolley

supermarket, spring morning

After a few days away, you come back and you have to do some shopping. Replenish the cupboards, the fridge, the freezer. You have no choice, as they say. It is one link in the chain of obligation which you cannot escape wearing, or at least not for very long, not in the grand style. Eating, washing, dressing, cleaning the house, doing the shopping. And as far as the latter goes, keeping an eye on the budget, comparing prices, shopping where you get more for less, or better for the same. Park your car, take a trolley.

Four wheels, a metallic cage, no brakes: the supermarket trolley. Vast capacity, intended to make one forget just how much. To be piled up with whatever can be drunk, eaten, read, listened to, carried. With all that is solid, liquid, whipped, frozen, synthetic, salted; with fruit and fish; with things that are visible, and others that are wrapped, packaged, hidden. The trolley is a thing of disorder and confusion. Of accumulation, miscellany, chaos. There are those who organise it mathematically, piles stacked to perfection, immaculately structured; and others who throw in one thing after another – a shambles of chocolate on ham on detergent on leeks on washing-up liquid. Either way, things get juxtaposed and chaos rules.

The trolley itself is, meanwhile, indifferent to all of this. Imperturbable. Forever wire-caged, forever metallic, forever on castors. Whatever its contents. Expressionless. Wherever it is left standing. Insensible to whatever is put inside it. Soulless. Any moment now you will start telling me that all things are like that – impassive, insensible. But in this case, with all the chaos going on in there, and everything piling up inside the cage of steel, that there should nevertheless reign such total detachment and imperturbability . . . The trolley must be a container in its purest form.

There come to mind, as I pass frozen foods, the words of Plato in *Pythagoras*: 'We run far more risk in our choice of acquaintances than in our choice of foods.' Because, Plato argues (between fruit and veg), you can see the merchandise on display before you purchase. You can feel it, you can judge it. With people, on the contrary, you take them untested into your heart of hearts. And if they are bad, you find yourself likewise damaged.

If we are not going to cut off our heads, as recommended earlier, and if we are to try and preserve a semblance of mind beneath the avalanche of things, perhaps we have to construct for ourselves a kind of soul-trolley. Metallic-grilled, well soldered, of light but rigid construction, which will keep its shape under pressure. A soul-receptacle on wheels, the same for everyone, able to be lined up and attached to its fellows. Indifferent to whatever is crammed into it, any old how, just like prefabricated, shrink-wrapped items thrown in one after another. Accustomed to being emptied at the checkout. Perhaps we need this metallic soul on wheels for the sole purpose of filling up and emptying, in constant succession. A soul not unlike the barrel of which Socrates (again) spoke, in his debate with Callicles in *Gorgias*. Our version does not fill up with rainwater, but with merchandise of all kinds. The model exists already. Our desire for things is incarnated in the very form and function of the supermarket trolley.

An announcement reverberates through the supermarket: 'Cleaning Service to the Men's Department.' It strikes me that this cannot be true. You cannot have men cleaned – not here, nor anywhere. Nobody can do that. Besides, it is not even desirable. Those who try, because they think they have the recipe, only make matters worse. All that remains for us is to keep pushing our trolley.

Dustbin

The rubbish is heavy to carry down. And the dust-bin which collects it is full every day. Like yours, no doubt. The sheer quantity of detritus produced daily by the average westerner is becoming signif-icant. Descending the stairs to deposit the plastic bag in the courtyard, I start thinking about the mode of being of a dustbin.

It seems fairly uncomplicated. The function of this particular thing is to collect refuse. It is the terminus for domestic things that have been dis-carded, expelled, written off. The place for cast-offs and scraps and trash. There is clearly a direct link between the supermarket trolley and the dustbin, with a brief detour of goods through the dining room or bathroom. The brevity of the detour gives rise to equally disposable reflections on the artificiality of modern life. Here is the place to deplore the vanity of our expenditure. I will happily dispense with doing so.

Discarded things do not cease to be things. They persist, on the contrary. Our decision to banish them may give us the feeling that they have been annihilated. But this is not quite the case. You know as well as I do that they endure. They may be tarnished, or in bits and pieces, or mouldy, I grant you. But they continue to exist and to commingle with each other. In the next world of the dustbin, the afterlives of things pursue their courses. In these basements and these rubbish chutes, there is no nothingness. Rather, a world bursting with fullness. The contents of the plastic bag I am carrying down, roughly, were I to open it: yoghurt wrapper, ripped in two; eggshells; leftovers of rice; tea-leaves; an empty bottle; newspapers; some tissues; used envelopes; peel (various); and at the bottom a mass of stuck-together things that I can no longer bear to identify. All in a scrum, every which way, higgledy-piggledy. The rule of disorder. In fact, the same principle as the supermarket trolley, but in reverse: as *output*. Evicted, banished to outer darkness. To the paradise of bad things, in effect. The universe of all that reeks. Of all that is fermentation, runoff, sourness, sagging, disintegration. A prospect to gladden the hearts of those eaters of vile things, the remote tribe in the opening pages of Flaubert's *Salammbô*.

Take a closer look. Stop telling yourself that those things that have overstayed their welcome in your life are magically spirited out of existence. Or those things that have ceased to sparkle and please you. All the putrefying things, the broken, ageing, threadbare, worn-out things; all those edifices of wrapping, of appearance, those ephemeral containers – all of it continues to accumulate somewhere else. I look with pity on the gaily-coloured carton which contained my wild-fruit yoghurts. An absurd reaction. Or perhaps not. It merely mirrors the absurd existence of the carton itself. Graphic designers designed it, printers proof-read it, hygienists controlled it, machines glued it together, storekeepers inventoried it, employees displayed it; from where it was checked out, deposited in my bag, placed in my refrigerator, and the following morning, in the space of two seconds, torn apart for the extraction of a yoghurt, and then tossed away.

Billions upon billions of things are thus flung away each day without a backward glance. Things which emerge from the void only to return thither without ever being so much as noticed. Which is why I am now giving them the benefit of my compassion. And why is it oddly difficult to avoid this trap of feeling? Probably because the same fate awaits us too: the falling apart, the stench, the being consigned to a plastic bag – ineluctably, definitively, ingloriously. And not just we ourselves, as individuals and organisms, but our works, our groups, our societies, our civilisations. Our knowledge, our experience. All of it, one day, in the dustbin.

It's not that this evening I suddenly discover the dustbin to be the destiny of our world. None the less, at this moment I can find no solace in the thought. In fact, I am not sure how to endure it. This damned bag I am carrying feels heavier and heavier.

Photocopier

One relatively recent mode of escape from the
dustbin of history: photocopy everything. Nothing
dies any longer, because everything is duplicated.
Is this the key to the coming order? The memory
of carbon paper, stencils, scanty and poor-quality
duplicates begins to fail us. Wherever you are,
unlimited copies of any document whatsoever
are now instantly obtainable. The photocopier,
unknown for millennia, has become indispensable. It retains nothing, creates nothing, neither
adds to nor subtracts from the available store of
reality. Its sole task: to duplicate. A machine that
knows only how to multiply, identically and indefinitely, whatever text or image is placed before it.
Give it one, and it makes two, or three, or twenty,
or one thousand, on and on.

In the days when copy clerks existed, such

individuals did not duplicate a text. They wrote a new text, line by line and word for word. Of course, this second text was supposed to be rigorously identical to the first. But this was never the case. Never. Not merely by reason of minuscule discrepancies in the writing, minute orthographic disparities, a loop here, a tiny erasure there. It was never the same text because the copyist, no matter how careful and attentive, no matter how adept and experienced, inevitably made mistakes: a word skipped here, a sentence misread there, an accent out of place.

The printing press put a stop to all of that. No more differences between one copy and the next – as long as they were from the same press and the same impression, of course. What this still necessitated were specialised workshops, guilds, warehouses for storage. Multiplication – the miracle of the loaves and the fishes – remained the province of experts, professionals, tradespeople. The individual was still kept out of the loop.

The photocopier put a stop to all of that. It opened the era of home proliferation. Anyone at all, without qualifications, without training, without knowledge, but in a position to push a button, can now duplicate whatever document comes to hand, in private, in the piracy of their own home, without asking anything of anyone. Brought within reach of us all, the photocopier has already produced, in one or two generations, billions and billions of copies. Behind the apparent banality of the statistic, let us not forget that the photocopier also inaugurated the whole era of duplication: CD-ROMs, DVDs and their clones . . . or that disks and photographs and films are the first cousins of the photocopier. Place someone on the glass, select the number of copies desired, press the button lightly, wait for the bright light and you can obtain the number of identical persons you require. For if we can make identical copies of texts, of music, of still or moving images, of sheep, of calves, why not of people too? Different technology? The technology will happen. Suffice that there exists the same conceptual mechanism, the same underlying matrix.

Soon the whole planet will smell of photocopier – that acid odour, vaguely pungent and headache-ish, which sometimes reminds one of the smell of a corpse, and yet is different. An odour of nothing, produced through surfeit, through multiplication. There are many ways to vanish. One is by extinction: I am no more. Another is by excess: I am too many, a thousand, a thousand thousand, a thousand thousand thousand.

Is the only solution to sabotage them all? The photocopier is a machine of feeble efficiency. Most of the time it is out of order. Might this be our only chance? For when these things become reliable, it will be the end. But the end of what exactly?

Wheelbarrow

in the country, early spring

I am trying to stay calm, without much success. Everywhere I turn there are things, and they seem to be on the increase. Every moment of the day, there they are, waiting to be deciphered. I have the impression of turning into an explanation machine, and one that is switched permanently on. With no off position, no means of disconnection. Even at night, the light is on inside my head. And it does not stop turning things over. So another attempt to find rural calm is in order, this time a long weekend.

The garden needs my attention. The earth is still heavy, loamy and compacted. The time for sowing is a while off yet, but now is a good moment for digging, filling in, rethinking the flowerbeds. I get the wheelbarrow out of the shed. It is not, alas, a wooden barrow, with tall sides and an iron-rimmed wheel, the like of which I knew as a child, when my father would ferry me together with the walnuts he had just gathered, and everything – the unripe walnuts and sour apples – smelt so powerfully of autumn. No, this wheelbarrow is metallic and green, with slightly silly flared sides, and a proper tyre; comfortable, mass-produced.

I feel a degree of loyalty towards it. I note moreover that the feelings of humans for wheelbarrows have not been sufficiently investigated. Simple machines that channel and transform our energy, of the pulley-and-lever variety . . . do they excite our gratitude by reducing our effort, or excite our pride by increasing our power? They allow us to do more with less effort, dividing our labour, making us mechanically efficient. The wheelbarrow belongs to this category. But there is something more: there is the wheel itself, that invention of genius, entirely simple and entirely perfect, which has changed the course of human history and modified the face of the world. I also admire the wheelbarrow for making the hub bear the weight of the load. I love the whole pitching and balancing of it, and the oscillations of the journey, when your stretched arms are weighed down by the load of earth you are ferrying and you can no longer tell which of you is doing the driving: the wheel or your legs, the thing or the person. It amuses and amazes me that this burden moves forwards despite everything pitching and tossing, veering this way and that.

Then suddenly the landscape itself seems to tip over. We are no longer in this sleepy garden. The wheelbarrow is pushing forward through night and mist. The images are in black and white, and they are flickering. On this thing of autumn leaves and potting sheds I now see corpses, piles of emaciated bodies, skeletal, barely human. These heaped carcasses are being tipped over into a ditch, buried in quicklime. My parents were adults when these countless piles of bones were being transported thus, barely covered in skin, a head or an arm bouncing in rhythm to the movement of the wheelbarrow, then tossed casually over into the pit. It sometimes happens that we are suddenly caught up by the past. Above all when the past is so recent.

Even the gardens are no longer at peace. Henceforth, two images of the wheelbarrow coexist, or one reversible image: life and death, well-being and horror. And nothing to separate them. At any time and in any place, the quiet of our days may topple over into the abyss without warning. Between one version of the world and another, only the hub of a wheel to take the strain.

Scythe

in the country, still early spring

I wake in a cold sweat, bolt upright. Not yet convinced about finding myself back again in the supposedly real world, so flat and unremarkable, but already relieved to know that absolute fear is, for the moment at least, only a dream. The scenario comes directly out of Edgar Allan Poe's 'The Pit and the Pendulum'. I am tied down on a bed, unable to move. Leather manacles hold my wrists and ankles, perhaps my neck too, I am no longer sure. From the ceiling, very high, very far away, an immense scythe-shaped blade sweeps downwards, at regular intervals, with a smooth pendulum movement. Shortly, sooner or later, it will slice into my throat. Unavoidably. Irreversibly. There is no way out. The nightmare is in the waiting. In following with my eyes the slow and ponderous motion of the pendulum. In hearing more and more distinctly the swish of the blade as it slices through the air. In knowing that to scream out or to attempt to struggle is pointless. I can make out in the gloom the exact moment when a ray of light flashes on the blade each time and then is gone; flashes and then is gone. I can anticipate, with a shuddering in the marrow of my being, the action of the slender blade as it opens a path through my flesh. In the dream. In reality, I have a particular horror of evisceration, of throat-cuttings, knife fights. The razor slicing through the human eye in *Un chien Andalou*. Death by intimate self-division, something very different from being crudely wiped out, blown up, drowned, burned to death. Instead, something silent, rapid, at first almost painless, leaving the flesh throbbing and separated from itself.

I am aware that the scythe has other associations too. Of harvest time. Ears of corn bowed over the fecund earth, the calloused hand of the peasant gripping the shaft, the rhythmic swaying of the whole body, a quarter turn upon oneself and then the return, as the golden corn rains down in the glow of summer. The scythe is linked both to Mother Earth and the grim reaper. Of binding and loosing. Life, and the end of life. Between these two, only a futile peasant's revolt, a *Jacquerie* without tomorrow, scythes brandished by a crowd of about-to-be-defeated rioters.

No one really uses scythes any more. As an object it is encountered only in the occasional storeroom, or disused cellar, or museum. It is a set of vanishing customs, along with what they might be said to symbolise. At the same time as the scythe disappears, there disappear from our everyday life the imagery of the harvest, the iconography of death, the memory of the riots staged by poverty. Today the scythe only swings in faraway places. In the countries of sweat and blood – Rwanda of the machetes, South America, Pakistan. Above all, it swings inside our heads. For there are mental things that are no less real, nor any less solid, than those against which we stub our toes or cut our fingers. They are probably more resistant, harder and purer, than those in the outside world. Possibly more menacing. Witness the archaic present tense of the cutting tool. A thing capable of dividing, of cutting clean through flesh, whether animal or vegetable. An antique thing which speaks of sacrifice and murder. Which belongs, mutely, to the realm of the gods and the division of spoils. A blade always preserves the trace of the last murder and the promise of the next. Such a tool does not figure in any collection or category because it divides and separates and carves up the categories.

I am not entirely sure what all of this might mean. It is possible that actual knives are always making up for Lichtenberg's celebrated, if notional, knife without a blade for which there is no handle. We have replaced the handle and replaced the blade, and we think that these things are knives. But in reality?

Statue

in a museum, Sunday

A quick trip abroad. I am invited by the philosophy department of a university to talk about my
research, research being one of the compartments
of my life. You too have compartments; no need to
describe mine, a rather peculiar concern, a spe-
ciality, having little obvious connection with the
world of things. Except for the journey itself, and
the way in which ordinary things change as soon
as you leave behind the customs of your own country, no matter how small the distance involved.
Abroad, the very first things I encounter, in the
first café, simply do not exist in my country: a
metal sugar container with a long spoon and a lid;
a small table dispenser for tiny squares of paper
which act as napkins. The list could go on and on.
All voyages, by definition, effect a mutation in
the world of things: different materials, modes of

use, locations, ways of being. Small differences, infinitesimal discrepancies, out of which is created the reality of elsewhere.

This morning, a few hours of freedom. A long walk along the quays, to the museum, whose name I already forget, on account of what I am about to experience there. It will be closing soon, just enough time left for a brief visit. First floor, the end room, right then left, unless I am mistaken. Along the way, some notable primitives, the usual triptychs and reredoses, but nothing to bowl one over or send one into raptures. Then suddenly, face to face with this thing, high up there in the entrance as I walk in. A sense of fear that I have never before experienced. I am transfixed, unable to breathe, as if my blood has frozen in its course. An unfamiliar and terrible sensation. The surroundings seem to fall away from me; nothing is left other than this statue, immense, its finger pointing. Uncertain whether it is alive or not, I remain as if petrified for a long interval, unable to make the smallest movement. The angel gazes at me. His stature overwhelms me; I do not understand what is happening, why this thing should possess so much presence – in other words, why it should seem not to be a thing. I start repeating to myself: 'It's only wood, it's only wood.' Trying to fend off the panic that is rooting me to the spot. At the same time there passes through my mind the expression 'every angel is terrible', which must be a phrase of Rilke, I no longer remember.

Nor am I entirely certain how everything manages to unfreeze again, allowing me to take refuge in the adjoining room. I still have difficulty breathing, but at least I have the sense of being out of reach. I recover my spirits. Exactly so: my spirits, which were no longer in my control. For what reason? I have no idea. But something to do with this thing of wood, evidently, just on the other side of the wall. A thing which borrows the human form, which simulates our scale, which works hard, by its posture and bearing, to pass for a fellow creature. Is that reason enough? Or else, leaving aside my individual pathology, is there an unreason particular to works of art? Ought they to be looked upon as things that possess an especial power, interfused with their physical being, their form, their materials, their very colours? What kind of power? What is it, integral to this statue, that is capable of bringing me suddenly to this halt? Its soul? But that is just another name for our ignorance.

At any rate, there exists a nation of things which are not to be confused with other things. Things which are possessed of a certain power, whether works of art or sacred objects; things invested with fantasy, with desires; things charged with messages; things so full of meaning that they are constantly overflowing their banks.

Questions III

There is a problem with this experiment. Which is that it is slowly suffocating me. Perhaps I am trying to cross an impossible barrier, exhausting myself to arrive at a point which I know in advance to be unreachable, by definition. I am not yet certain if the impossibility is inherent in the project as such, or in the manner in which I have set about it. There is something unusual and perhaps irrational about the question underlying the experiment: to find out how things are is a peculiar undertaking. On the other hand, it does not seem to me impossible to imagine an answer, nor does there seem to be any-thing inherently dangerous about the search. So it must be the manner in which I have gone about it. But which aspect? I make an effort broadly to retrace my steps. But will this necessarily tell me where I went astray?

Before I began the journey, if I am not mistaken, no object excited my particular surprise, every thing I encountered was effortlessly labelled and assimilated. They were all in order, all in their proper places. As far as I can recall, I used to perceive the object world and the diversity of its contents as a single whole, more or less uninterrupted, smooth, relatively featureless, occasionally reassuring and (above all) created for my own personal use. As I gradually began to look at things differently – these things so close to hand, so easy to pick up or merely to brush lightly against, ever present, always within reach – these hitherto ordinary objects began to distance themselves steadily, so as often to seem unreachable and ultimately impenetrable. For several months (how many? eight? nine? I do not rightly know) I have been moving in this half-light, wherein an unthinking familiarity combines with the most disconcerting sense of estrangement.

As if another face keeps surfacing in the familiar reflection. Even the simplest of things, the most reassuring, reveal an untamed depth, inhuman, inexpressible. Between me and them I perceive more and more clearly that there exists an uncrossable abyss. Does my error consist in nevertheless wanting to cross it? These voiceless things, inert and oblivious, are the unfeeling denizens of a world with no connection to mine. I describe them incorrectly as having a wherever to inhabit; they are in fact entirely devoid of a world. And I shall never make contact with them. Even thinking of such a possibility, I have the sense of moving into a more rarefied atmosphere. At bottom, I no doubt believe myself capable of stepping outside my own head. Which is an error and also a source of exhaustion.

Do things speak? Do they have something to say? Is it not simply we (as always) who attribute senses to them, and a possible language? No, it is not quite as simple as that. We make things speak, but only by acting on particulars innate to them. Things neither truly speak nor are they entirely speechless. But the dream of entering into silence, into brute matter, and seeing the world from the viewpoint of things, carries its dangers. To fall prey to this illusion is to become dust with the dust, with no possibility of return.

Faced with this impasse, perhaps we need to create a new relationship, establish a new kind of distance. Neither indifference towards things, nor fascination. Neither language nor silence. Neither fear nor false expectation. We need to discover a different route. But how? This is not something I can answer, I merely glimpse the possibility of a new *status quo*, a new equanimity.

It is certainly futile to fear things. Let us shake off all those phantasms of being suffocated by the world of objects. They replicate only because we desire them to do so. One can always discard encumbrances. So let us stop inventing nightmares about the teeming accumulation of things. They are without connection to each other, without volition or intention, even without number, in the strict sense of the term. Let us silence the gnawing voice inside us, protesting that things are taking over our space, claiming our time, encumbering our spirit, enlisting our bodies, threatening our lives. Let us stop parading images of surfeit, of blockage, of chaos.

Otherwise, we must draw the inevitable conclusion that the masters of the world, today, are things. In which case, humanity is no longer anything more than a tiny minority, practically deprived of rights or agency. Our species, until recently still considered to be intelligent, articulate and industrious, has lost control. Things have become exponentially more numerous than people. They are almost without exception longer lasting, more robust, more reliable. Have not their demographic expansion, their longevity, their staying power, their capacity for organisation and their diversity got the better of our human (all too human) fecklessness and failings?

Shall we concede that things henceforth and irrevocably hold the keys to our individual experience as well as our collective enterprise? They regulate everything, without appearing to do so. Absolutely everything. Our least actions are conditioned by legions of seemingly docile things. Our movements, our wishes, our work and our play, the fabric of our everyday life – all are dependent on things, their abundance or rarity, their functionality. This reign of things is without flaw and without alternative. There is no escape, no elsewhere.

One might go so far as to maintain that the perspective of the object-world is in many respects more valuable than our own. That things are better than people. They are unquestionably simpler and more serene than you or I. They are categorically more virtuous. You might say that they are incomparably freer and fairer than we are, although 'free' and 'fair' are approximate human categories, imperfectly adapted to the sovereign stringency of things. It might be going too far to maintain that we cannot arrive at the essence of things, since they have no such attribute, but at this point we may as well envisage a Universal Declaration of the Rights of the Thing. Decidedly, it is time to try and follow some other trails.

CALM

When a man lets himself be blinded by things, he consorts with the dust. When a man lets himself be dominated by things, his heart is troubled. A troubled heart can only produce a laborious and rigid stroke of the brush, and sows its own destruction . . . Therefore I leave things to commingle with the darkness of things, and dust to associate with dust; therefore is my heart untroubled, and when the heart is untroubled, painting can begin.

Shitao,
*Remarks on Painting
by the Monk Bitter-Pumpkin*

Flute

at home, spring morning

It happens every year. Each morning it gets light earlier and earlier, and for a few weeks I dig in my heels, burrow underneath the covers, do everything I can to stay hibernated. Then one morning everything changes: my pattern of sleep switches over to summer time, to waking with the dawn, to a life ruled by light. It happens without transition, and so abruptly that each time I remain astonished by it, as is the case this morning.

The sky is so clear that I am impelled to get out my flute. Which I don't know how to play. It has remained, for me, a silver-plated tube, with stops and valves of an unforgiving precision. I have never reached that point where the thing comes to life and becomes resonant instead of ponderous. No matter; I persist with it none the less. Or rather, I continue along a different route. I long ago abandoned the dream of being able to play, even modestly – even less than modestly. I continue without hope, almost without purpose, just for the pleasure of the thing. For sound and breath combined, for the delicate vertigo of it, the Aeolian ecstasy.

Those things which are intended for music-making form a tribe apart. Their relationship to the body is altogether singular. They lay down their terms, and at the same time expect the body to do all the work. The flute demands a very particular posture of the torso and positioning of the arms and fingers; an exact application of lips and of breath. A few millimetres changes everything. A little more or a little less breath, tip of tongue, pressure of lips, prominence of teeth, presence of saliva, and inclination of head; a little more or less suppleness of thumb and pressure of fingers; above all, a little more or less self-presence, focus, cohesion – and the entire scenery shifts as from one world to another. From the ethereal to the mired, or conversely from the mud to the empyrean. Despite all of which, it would be far too simplistic to assume that the body merely submits to the musical instrument, that it alone bows to the many and simultaneous dictates of the instrument. No, the body after all wakens the instrument, brings it out of its inert and mute condition, brings it to life and opens its eyes to its living self.

What is most moving about this is the necessarily workaday nature of the encounter between object and body. Without the instrument, no amount of musculature and tendons and finger joints can make music, which the instrument alone makes possible. But without the body, no amount of metal or pipes or stops or reeds or strings will ever produce the least sound, which the instrumentalist alone calls into being. Never the one without the other. And yet each owes everything to the existence of the other. They both give and receive, complete each other and realise themselves through each other. Impossible to know which plays and which is played upon, whether the person plays the instrument or the instrument the person. They play each other and upon each other, in which consists the unceasing miracle of music making.

No doubt the grammar of gesture and posture is infinitely various. According to the instrument, the repertoire, the epoch, the civilisation; according to how you blow, strike, touch, pluck or strum. What remains identical, however, at the heart of this infinite variety, is the acoustic and rhythmic union of person and thing. This alliance is at the origins of life. Let us not forget what the first flutes were made of: hollowed-out tibias pierced with holes, old femurs made resonant. There is in the musical instrument a gesture that transcends death: a recycling of bones, a bringing back to life of bodies that have become things. This gesture is universal in history, whatever the time or the place: there is no record of a human group or society without music.

Might this provide a possible way out of our impasse? Might we transcend our anomie, in respect of things, by taking the musical thing as our model? What would happen if we behaved towards each thing as if it were a musical instrument? Would we play them all? What tunes would we play? Where would the score be found? Would we need to improvise?

It is time for me to clean my flute. Too much saliva always seems to get into it.

Necklace

restaurant, foretaste of summer

A couple of hours are sufficient. A wind coming from the south, and suddenly the warmth is here, and more than the warmth itself, even a hint of dog days to come. I invite the woman I love to dinner, outside, under the trees. It seems a long time since we have been outdoors together in the softness of the evening, far too long. This breath of warm air is like a holiday; the lights will come on shortly, like the promise of a dance.

I like to see her in many sorts of places, whether here or abroad, in our haunts and familiar places as much as in places unfamiliar to one or even both of us. I like waiting for her in a particular place, knowing that she will appear, with her air of being on time by chance. I like meeting her in public places, picking her out in the crowd, spotting her in the middle of the crush. I like to watch her coming from afar, elegant and slender, with that air of being at once confident and, secretly, a little lost. I like the exact moment when our eyes meet, that glow of recognition, wherever we may be. Neither the months nor the years nor our innumerable rendezvous can diminish the intensity of that moment.

She is wearing a black dress, simple and beautiful. I wonder for a moment which is darker, the dress, her eyes or her hair. Then suddenly I notice the necklace. It is just like her to think of wearing it, on this summery night, in the warm air so evocative of the Greek island where I gave it to her, the first time we celebrated her birthday.

The point of which, and the only aspect of either the necklace or the evening in question that is remotely relevant to the matter in hand, is this: it serves to remind me that there exists a very particular category of things, to which this necklace quite clearly belongs. 'Jewels' or 'finery' do not communicate the reality, or barely so. More like things for skin, body things, finely worked things, for display. In one sense useless, in another sense they are of a higher or even supreme utility. It has nothing to do with money or wealth: these things are always widely encountered among peoples who lack everything. Whether Native Americans or nomads, oral cultures, pre-industrial societies without any concept of fashion – people without possessions, it seems, are never people without jewels. They cover their necks with necklaces, their wrists with bracelets.

These things of always and everywhere are nevertheless things exclusively of the here and now, worn by one individual, in intimate closeness to a particular area of skin. It is a subtle and special kind of interplay, as with music, between thing and person. Soundless, however. It revolves solely around display. But who is showing what? The necklace shows off the neck. Or does the neck show off the necklace? Or do they show off each other in exactly equal measure? Are other things also being intimated? The superfluity that enhances life? The sovereign vitality of things that serve no vital purpose?

It is worth holding on to the fact that historically the superfluous never comes second to the necessities of bare survival. There is no postponed state where – their needs satisfied and the continuity of the organism assured – humans turn to devising forms of aesthetic play and objects of luxury. Luxury is encountered amongst the most primitive peoples. It is present in the most archaic communities, the most materially destitute. We are a species of derailed monkey who, since the dawn of time, have celebrated, in continuous fashion, the indispensability of things that are entirely useless to our survival.

Umbrella

afternoon, in the city

In this country, it never stays warm for more than two or three days at a time. Then the thunderstorms arrive, followed by the squalls of wind; the temperature drops, everyone feels relieved. Then the rains come, and all is as it should be. People moan, they complain about the lousy weather, but at least this is normal and not disquieting, like those uncomfortable heat-waves that arrive from somewhere else, who knows from where. In short, umbrellas are once again the order of the day.

Now here is an object that can never be praised too highly. Ingenious, meticulous, industrious and provident, as if it were not content with being obliging, gallant and dependable. And a thing of wonder, to boot: when you observe closely the unfurling of an umbrella, paying close attention to the interaction of all the joints, the precisely calculated tension of the canopy, and the overall effect of this delicate metal structure as it opens into a corolla, you are witnessing one of the most instructive of spectacles. Albeit one of the least familiar, despite being available on demand to any inhabitant of the supposedly temperate regions of the earth. I'd say that the inventor of the umbrella, or perhaps the cohort of scrupulous spirits who perfected it over the ages, probably possessed a keen sense of aesthetics and equally of craftsmanship, as well as pince-nez, sideburns and red cheeks, slightly blotched in all probability. I have no idea if there are monuments in honour of him (or them). Are the historians interested? I presume so. If not, then they ought to be taking an interest. And in the unlikely case of an obscure origin, collective, anonymous, then we must invent an inventor . . .

The individual in question was clearly a poet. Nobody, in point of fact, has ever had any need of an umbrella. There were always roofs, covered arcades, dense foliage and – for exposed trips – all the necessary paraphernalia: hats, cloaks, greatcoats. The umbrella was never lacking, for it never corresponded to the slightest need. The spirit that conceived of the umbrella was responsible for more than a mere thing: she or he invented a portable roof, a private sky, a mobile refuge, all of which makes walking under the pouring rain an experience of shelter but also of reassurance, safe from the milky infinity above our heads. With next to nothing, the umbrella creates a world of extreme subtlety: enclosed but not locked in, protected but not confined, fixed yet mobile, constant but able to be furled away, as intermittent as rain and at the same time a permanent fixture.

Possibly the rain was merely a pretext. Many other things, as we have noted, do the business as far as protecting ourselves from the rain is concerned. It is not from water that the umbrella preserves us – the drips are merely props – but from the sky above. It offers us a small sky, opaque, portable, on a human scale. No more infinite spaces. No more gaping abyss, no more intrusion from on high. Nothing swooping down on us. Our gaze turned, finally, towards the earth. It has always seemed to me that one thinks better, incomparably so, under an umbrella.

Its final and greatest advantage: egoism. The umbrella forms a heaven for me alone, portable and made to measure. Moreover, it legitimises egoism and renders it harmless, which is a rare feat indeed. Was the inventor of the umbrella such a philanthropist as to find an acceptable excuse for separating us from our fellow men? Did he know that we are each other's rain?

Motor Car

on the road, one evening

In the past, a long time ago, or perhaps a very short time ago, things were motionless. All things, without exception. Set down, incapable of movement, waiting for a living force to transplant them, to shift them from one place to the next. Powerless, devoid of the slightest capacity for locomotion. Heavy, rigid, dense, withdrawn indefinitely into themselves. They could be moved, if necessary, conveyed through water, dragged by beasts of burden. But never did they move themselves. Never. It was simply unthinkable.

From this point of view, we have changed the world. We have given birth to things capable of moving themselves. Possessed of motive force, powerfully so. Trading places themselves, by their own energy, and transporting our bodies further and more rapidly than we could ever hope to achieve under our own steam, except in our dreams.

And yet, has the reality of this situation dawned on us yet? Evidently not. I get into my car, I start it up, move forwards, without any clear notion of being seated inside a thing which proceeds as I steer it, in my capacity as a human being seated inside a thing. Just as the soul is not inside the body, like the captain of a ship, but entirely commingled with the body, likewise the driver turns into the thing being driven, which – in turn – turns into the driver.

The car is no longer simply a thing, but a proxy for the body, an extension of one's power of motion. We wear this garment of power, this envelope of speed. The boundary between object and person becomes very fluid, very difficult to trace. 'I am parked in the next street,' he says to me, sitting in the restaurant. So where is he? On the chair in front of me, or in the next street? Is his body truly here, or truly there? His own words confess that he has no idea. His body is fluid. All our bodies are fluid.

Imagine a situation where all cars were suddenly banned. By an ecological dictatorship, a green Taliban regime, a fanatical zealotry of the archaic. Let us forget for a moment the unlikely scenario leading up to this sudden and categorical fatwa. Skeletons of cars would lie about rusting, and would slowly disintegrate. Heroic resistance fighters would salt away carburettors in caves whose location was known only to them. With a little ingenuity, one could doubtless invent the fiction of a world that reverted suddenly but naturally to walking and riding.

What one could not imagine, however, is what would happen to our bodies in such a world. How would people cope with coming down to earth again, with being landed back on their own two feet? How would they ever re-adapt to moving with slow steps, so ponderous suddenly, having known the lightness of the breeze, gliding this way and that, everywhere at once?

I am convinced that, in the event, there would be collective breakdown, mass suicide. People would feel as if their skulls were caving inwards and crushing their brains. For too long, motorised objects have taken us out of ourselves, and raised us above the ground. In the past – so long ago and yet so recently – humanity knew that it was impossible to fly. For us today it would be intolerable never to fly again, never to drive, never to be whirled about. We are not sure why it would be intolerable. And we give hardly any thought to this eventuality. Besides, it has practically no chance of coming about, anywhere in the world. We keep moving.

Suitcase

at home, afternoon,
end of winter

I am going to the country for a few days. Spring is already in the air. The light feels different. Some friends have lent me their house, on top of a hill, where the eye can travel far. It is a place to which I am very attached, where I feel calm, where I quite simply come back to earth.

Hence the suitcase in the hall. I see it as a friendly and reassuring thing, whereas in many people it induces anxiety. Perhaps I am too nomadic, or too sedentary: the sight of a suitcase gives me pleasure. Happy as I am to be for ever on the move, whether going or coming. Above all, the suitcase is for me a rational object. Square, solid, requiring us to take a minimalist view of our actual physical requirements. What reassures about the suitcase is that it is a small mobile house, which I carry in my hand, or roll along at my side. It is clearly impossible to fit everything in, to cart everything around. Impossible and superfluous. A choice is imposed by the suitcase, by its necessary limits. It is an exercise in composition. Concision, efficiency. The maximum of possibilities in the minimum of space. The sobriety of a life reduced to essentials, however temporarily. Bringing only what is necessary, with a touch of the superfluous, nonetheless, as a gesture. Just in case. One never knows. On the off-chance. Why not, if it will fit in?

The philosophical asceticism of the suitcase. A touch of the Epicurean about it, that the body has but few needs. Happiness is possible if desire is kept within the limited confines of the body. The dream of a world where each of us would have just one suitcase, a light suitcase, easy to carry. With everything inside. Everything he or she needs, everything he or she possesses, everything he or she values. Such a world would no doubt be a better world, easier to live in. But what am I saying, really?

Might it not, on the contrary, be the worst of possible worlds, an anti-world? There surges into view an image to freeze one's blood, of tens, hundreds, thousands, tens of thousands, hundreds of thousands of men, women and children each carrying their suitcase. An image from not so long ago. People who were the same age as my parents. They are taking a train. They are not coming back. Their suitcases are piled in heaps. They are murdered, burnt, reduced to ash. There are no words for this. No points of comparison. No reason. It still goes on. It is normal. It is incomprehensible.

Television Set

*Sunday evening,
in the country*

It is more obvious when the screen is switched off. Then you can see that it is an opaque object, a box of shadows. The rest of the time, what with the sound and colour, the constant flickering, the zapping and the channel hopping, it appears to be alive. You forget. But when you look at it switched off, it's a different thing altogether: a sombre cube, exuding a vague air of placidity, falsely familiar, even a little menacing. You cannot tell what might come out of this black box. Perhaps it is watching you; perhaps it is entirely harmless.

Again we are dealing with a screen and light – with consciousness, if you like – as with the computer. But here the codes are reversed. The computer has to do with white light, with awareness, the stimulus of sentences, choices, prompts, games, projects, calculations, inventions. The television on the other hand partakes of all colours without, however, ceasing to be black. Consciousness is in eclipse, it stagnates, it is mesmerised. Rendered completely passive. Ingurgitating motionlessly and unflinchingly whatever passes before it. The moving image captures the attention and paralyses it, focuses it, consumes it, divides and rules it. Our gaze is possessed, our body rendered vegetal, our thought processes stilled.

It is by no means disagreeable, the imagination placed on an instantaneous drip, with nothing to do and no escape. Taken in hand, and taken in by the editing, by the close-ups, by the manipulated images. It is by no means disagreeable, let me repeat, since that is precisely the worst of it, the key to the triumph of television, to its grip upon the world, more powerful today than any other mechanism for social control. We allow our heads to be filled with ready-made images, and the process is by no means disagreeable. A drip-feed releasing us from ourselves, from the burden of having to direct our own thoughts, from the requirements of being a body. Anaesthesia is intrinsic to the process of watching. They could make excellent programmes, they could inform, educate, cultivate, and it would make no difference – none of us would be awakened by any of it. Because it would only be a dream of waking in the midst of deep sleep.

Does anyone study the relationship between the expansion of television sets and the decline of political and social upheaval? Perhaps not. Certain conclusions can nevertheless be drawn. No major political revolution has occurred since the advent of television's universal hegemony. It is quite possible that there will be no more upheaval. The television set is not merely another instrument of domination, restraint or control. In a sense it does much more, and much more effectively: it causes you to be absent from your self, to be out when you are in. You think that the whole world has paid a visit to your living room. So it has. But you were out.

Sanding Machine

In this house where I live, I generally have several repair jobs in progress at any one time. According to circumstances, I find myself becoming a plumber, or a carpenter, or a tiler, or a mason, or a gardener, or even a roofer, all of which roles I learnt one by one and on the job, a long time ago, while renovating an old house of mine from top to bottom during the course of several years. The pleasure I take in these jobs reinforces my conviction that I am not a real intellectual. So much the better.

Since the present house belongs to friends, doing their odd jobs is also my way of thanking them. Taking a house in hand is always an emotional business, as though one were tending a living organism. Initially there is a certain amount of damage and annoyance. Like surgery, or dressing a wound. Then, if the operation takes, if everything heals, the house gets to lead a new life.

All morning I have been sanding the floorboards of a room fitted out in the attic. The sanding machine is a large industrial-sized drum model, which must be held quite flat to the ground and kept going at a constant speed to avoid making furrows in the wood. The noise is deafening, and I protect my ears with wax plugs to avoid hearing ringing noises for hours afterwards. I also need to protect my nose and mouth with a paper mask, so thick is the dust. As I steer the thing, a bright yellow cloud is raised, depositing infinitesimal wood shavings in my hair, eyebrows, lashes and all over my skin.

The motor, powerful but elderly, trembles and vibrates. The vibrations pass from my palm to my wrist, then my elbow, then my shoulder. Fairly soon my whole body is vibrating, letting itself be carried along to the high-pitched yet sonorous rhythm of this thing-machine. Little by little the floorboards change colour. The venerable patina of grime and varnish gives way to the matt dullness of the stripped wood. Things often act upon other things. Always so, in the case of tools. This sanding-thing transforms the floorboard-things, but in a very specific manner: the removal by abrasion of a very thin layer, which is capable – despite the airy thinness – of transforming its entire appearance.

Let us have no more roughness, I say. Let us live in the world of the smooth. The calm, soothed, clarified, cleansed surface. Would it not be a good thing if there were sanding machines for everything? Devices capable of scouring our ideas, of smoothing out our sentences, of levelling the surface of entire works. Would this be desirable? As a result of enduring so much vibration, dust and decibels, I have clearly lost my plot. Such machines have of course existed for centuries.

Vacuum Cleaner

When you do sanding, a fine film of dust settles everywhere, on every horizontal surface, even high up, on mouldings, window sills, door frames and panels. It gets right down into the smallest corners. Imperative to vacuum everywhere meticulously. Nothing gives me more pleasure than to see this fine, beige-yellow dust disappearing, millimetre by millimetre. The layer covering every moulding of the door simply vanishes, spirited away as the nozzle of the vacuum cleaner makes its progress. Even better: the hoovering has the effect of making the film of dust disappear *in advance of* the nozzle's progress, before it even reaches the dust as such. This all takes place in short order, and the room is briskly restored to its prior state.

The vacuum cleaner is an intriguing specimen of animal-thing. From a continuous little high-pitched cry to a strident tone of unmodulating complaint, its voice changes according to the underlay, the materials, the types of flooring. With its long, flexible trunk and insatiable voracity, the vacuum cleaner is a mechanical pig equipped for the tropics, a sort of ravenous clockwork Ganesh. It has bad breath, much of the time. Of its gluttonous nature there can be no doubt. Try placing the end of its trunk anywhere on your skin. Your flesh is instantly lifted, caught up, distended, while the belly of the beast emits a stifled groan of hunger and satisfaction combined, which does not bode well. Can you not see yourself being hoovered whole in an instant, and disappearing along with everything else? But conveyed to where? Were it not for that question, the vacuum cleaner would merely be an amusing and utile thing, rather than an aid to reflection.

In fact, few household things give as much pause for thought as the vacuum cleaner. It is on the side of everything that is clear and distinct. When everything is crumbs and fluff, it restores the domestic stage to its pristine condition. Even when you have no desire to start hoovering, is not your pride in restoring the domestic stage a powerful motive? There is of course a further dimension: that we are dust, and unto dust we shall return. The crucial point: we are all hoover material, fodder for the nozzle and the flexible tube, all destined for blackout in the great dust bag of the cosmos. Who empties it out? Where does all the dust go? Does it sometimes make a little metallic jingling noise in the tube, as buttons and paperclips and other sorts of pins sometimes do when they are passing through?

I imagine the process as never-ending. One by one, along with the dust, the lightest things all get sucked up. Then the things of average weight, then the heavy things. The world itself disappears. In its place, gradually, a beautiful void extends its reign. The entire universe is vacuumed. A clean sweep is made of the whole of time – at last. The turmoil is over. Everything has gone. There remain only a few questions: if this is the case, how do I know it to be so? A secondary consideration: what of the after-sales service? And metaphysically speaking: good riddance?

Bicycle

country road,
summer morning

I know it by heart, this stretch of ten kilometres separating the house from the sea. A long straight, except for the zigzag that skirts the last farm before the dunes; then the descent towards the shoreline once past the long, slow incline. It is best experienced by bicycle. But first of all I have to get the machine going, remove the layers of dust, pump up the tyres, check the brakes, test the saddle, grease the cogwheels. Every time I tinker with a bicycle I think of the nineteenth century. This object belongs to that age. Even if it was only perfected subsequently, the idea of the bicycle has all the hallmarks of those engineers of tubular steel. Their understanding of mechanics and equilibrium: accuracy of calculation, simplicity of end result. The bicycle is first cousin to the railway, the steam engine, the architectures of metal. It always has an air of stepping directly out of an old engraving, a drypoint, a line drawing, something in black and white in the pages of magazines before photography. At once restrained and over-elaborated.

It is a form which hides its function. Before riding it, you can easily get the impression that this assemblage of scrap iron will never get going. Thrown together – approximate, hit or miss. Not to mention heavy. However, it is enough to ride ten feet to experience something quite different: a gliding sensation, airy, precise, flowing. The bicycle is two different beings – in repose and in movement. In movement, all its attributes are radically transformed. From this point of view, there is something of the musical instrument about the bicycle: a metamorphosis of both object and person which occurs only in and through their mutual encounter.

Above all, it is a thing of equilibrium and of movement. At rest, it collapses. It only stays upright for as long as it is moving forwards; it can never stop if it is to continue being itself. Very few objects are in this category: the hoop and the spinning top, those other nineteenth-century props that accompanied the children of the rich, along with governesses and private parks. To devise, manufacture and spread the word about a vehicle propelled by human agency alone, and functioning only on condition that it is kept moving – all this required the nineteenth century. The age of capital, of belief in science, of historical progress. All three of which resemble the bicycle: they exist only in so far as they keep moving.

I am about to broach the slow incline that precedes the descent to the sea. The sky is milky, the lower air is warm. A feeling of utter ease sweeps over me. The bicycle characteristically makes one forget about the movements required to keep it going. As I change gears, I think there is a lesson here, relating to epistemology. What 'knowledge', after all, is required to ride a bicycle? Almost nothing that can be usefully explained or described. Almost nothing communicable. No manuals, no brochure even. Just a sort of confidence in the reality of movement and in its dogged continuity, plus a physical realignment which the body discovers of its own accord and never forgets. This knowledge is either complete or completely absent: nobody knows how to ride by halves, or is two-thirds able to ride.

Meanwhile, I am beginning to get out of breath. Fortunately, the descent towards the sea is coming very soon. I savour the moment when, just as your muscles begin to ache and your heart is thumping, all effort suddenly disappears, and you have only to coast downhill, holding your course with barely a glance at the road. The sky is still white, the sea a pale grey on the horizon, not a breath of wind, calm before the storm. The bicycle flies along soundlessly, without activity, a pure vector, as if immobile at the very heart of movement. This will never end, I think. I will be descending this slope thus, indefinitely, for eternity, century after century. It sometimes happens that we escape from time. Just for a moment, if I can express it thus. As a unit of time, it lasts but a few instants, or a few minutes, nothing more than a lapse. But being outside of time is by definition measureless. Without duration. And it is by this means that we humans have access to eternity. Not by living for ever, but by being able sometimes, on rare occasions, to ride out of time.

Cable

They arrive punctually, efficiently, impersonally. These are the cable men, who connect you and link you up. When they arrive, they immediately walk the course. They establish the best way of connecting the cable to your apartment. Then they feed it out and fasten it. Finally, they set it functioning. And there you are, on line, wired up. Connected, physically, to the entire network. What passes through this cable is infinitely various: electrical energy, conversations, images, sound, texts, messages. As we all know.

Since the cable men came just now to install a high-speed connection, I have been reflecting on this peculiar stuff called cable. Cables in general – the most common variety, electrical or phone cables – are probably the most ubiquitously widespread of all hidden things. They are everywhere: in the floor, the walls, the ceilings, under the streets, under the oceans, in rich countries and poor countries, cold countries and warm countries. Cable is the most evenly distributed thing in existence. Remove cable, and at a stroke you make the world in which we live disappear: no more electricity, no television, no telephone, no internet. It is true that more and more links dispense with its services, preferring satellite or radio relay. But these account for only a tiny proportion of the network, which remains dependent on the existence of a multi-coloured multitude of cables. Whole families of cables, entire tribes of cables, with their diverse functions, thicknesses, colours and textures.

All these cables form a web of connections, at once tangible and invisible, between people. No one in practice gives them any thought. Imagine, however, if you were to feel your way along the telephone wire, you would end up by meeting the person to whom you are speaking, whether they are in Seoul or in Sydney, in Buenos Aires or in Vancouver. The species of thing called cable, which begins to be threatened here and there, has for the past two centuries known a demographic explosion for which there is no equivalent. At the start of the nineteenth century, there existed not a single specimen of this class of thing. Today they are to be found on every continent, billions upon billions of them. One could write a history, and above all a topography, of cable, retracing the manner in which this thing conquered the world and left its imprint everywhere. One would have to explain how it engendered enterprises, how it mustered experts and surveyors, engineers and navvies. The history of modern times merges with that of the cable, which can be used to reconstruct modernity almost in its entirety.

But in what respect can the existence of cable be said to induce calm? Because it allows us to think of our loved ones as being 'reachable'? Because it weaves across the earth an unending tracery which reminds us of the veins, arteries, nerves and wiring of a huge living organism? Because this colossal entanglement transmits speech instantaneously? No, there is another and more important reason. What is reassuring about the existence of cable is its rubbery banality. The worlds that it transmits may be as virtual as we could wish, but it remains first and foremost through a wire, whether single or braided, metal or glass, that this everything is transmitted. Through sewers and over roofs and under the pavements of the city, through the stairwell, up the walls and into the very frame of your own front door. Which is, in effect, a reassuring thought.

Spirit Level

With the arrival of summer, things quieten down.
I begin to sort through piles of books, mail and
papers that have been unattended to for weeks and
weeks. I decide to run up some new bookshelves
in the corridor, to try and check the growing disorder of my workroom. An opportunity to become
reacquainted with my friend of long standing, the
spirit level. For those who are – shame on you –
ignorant of this implement, I will remind you quickly: it is a sort of flat ruler into which is inserted a
small glass tube, filled with water or oil, in which
there appears a bubble. To ensure the horizontality
of a shelf, it suffices to lay this ruler on top. The
shelf is level when the bubble is exactly centred
inside the glass tube, between the two lines calibrated on the glass. There do exist, of course,

spirit levels that allow you to control, by means of a similar device, the verticality of a post, a partition, a door frame and so on. There even exist – to which I am especially partial, for the usual obscure reasons – double spirit levels, which allow one to control both the horizontal and vertical planes simultaneously.

Nothing is more instructive than a spirit level, should you wish to establish just how disconcerting – far more than we think – the three-dimensional universe is. Suppose, in effect, that you have managed to put up a shelf that is perfectly horizontal. It tilts neither to the left nor the right. Exemplary and virtuous, it holds itself proudly parallel to both floor and ceiling (assuming, for an optimistic moment, that these two planes are themselves horizontal). Just as you feel rising within you a legitimate pride in this victory over matter, this triumph of the spirit over the world of things, you suddenly become aware that your shelf leans either backwards or forwards: admirably level on the left-to-right axis, it tilts abominably on the front-to-rear axis.

The spirit level puts you in control of this situation. It guides you, irrespective of the inconsistencies of the floor, the flaws in the walls. It traces the horizontal as surely, as unfailingly, as the compass indicates true north, or as the tuning fork gives us an A. The spirit level belongs to this family, relatively limited, of things that offer points of reference. In themselves, they are close to the degree zero of usefulness. But they give orders to other things, organising their lives and arranging them. And this organising character designates them as things of pure rationality. The spirit level plays this role to perfection. It introduces into the world a principle of straightness. It surveys and corrects, submitting other things to an abstract rule. It embodies the norm and realises it, imposes it on a recalcitrant world which insists on remaining squint or lopsided.

The spirit level is a thing that regulates, a force for order. It is akin to other yardstick-things, things that serve as measures and which establish themselves as the point of reference when everything else goes to hell. I am reminded of the case of the standard metre that was elected to serve as the model for all other standard metres, which was cast in platinum-iridium alloy and housed in some scientific institution or other: rendered official and precious. As a child I found this deeply reassuring, that the platonic metre should be permanently deposited somewhere, guarded and looked after. But what of the spirit level? Where can we find horizontality deposited? In which institution?

As I finish attaching the shelves between the verticals, it occurs to me that a spirit level could be invented for our actions. How can we know if an action is moral or otherwise? Might this be the solution? Might Kant have invented the spirit level of practical reason?

Table

I find the spirit level lying on a table in the dining room. How did it get there? Perhaps I laid it there on my way to answer the phone? I no longer remember. But I notice from the bubble that the table is not level. It leans noticeably to the left. No matter. No one seems to have noticed until now. Besides, whereas a shelf has to be exactly horizontal, a table is under no such obligation. Because a table is not a thing so much as a thing-world. It has no single use, but a multitude of uses. It is the thing which most clearly marks, at least in the West, the constitution of a human space. Instead of eating and working on the ground, or on his knees, man has laboured to establish a flat and uniform surface, raised, parallel with the ground – a second ground, so to speak, at the level of our activities.

The table is an intermediate surface, which gets us off the ground but maintains our link to the ground; which parallels the natural world with a human plane. This second world is the place of study, of work, of business; the place of meal-taking, of the family, of all that is utile as well as all that is festive. The space of friends, of knights of Round Tables, trade unionists at the negotiating table, banquets on Olympus, the Last Supper, the end of Asterix's adventures. In the West, the table conceives of all historical events as moments punctuating everyday life.

Imagine, for a few seconds, that an as yet inconceivable virus were to smite all the tables in the world tomorrow and destroy them one and all. Without exception. Low tables as well as high tables, round as well as square as well as rectangular, nests of tables as well as garden tables, bridge tables, kitchen tables, night tables, work tables and conference-room tables. The lot, in short. Imagine, from one day to the next, a world without tables, a humanity without tables. Think of the damage this would do. Imagine the upheavals. Try and measure the extent of the cataclysm. Suddenly you are eating on the ground, papers and keyboards cover the carpet, you no longer know where to put anything, people are losing their heads and arguing with each other, wars are brewing over here, others have already broken out over there, negotiations are grounded, nothing works, no one can be brought to the table: there is no table.

So, give thanks to tables for their unfailing presence, everywhere reliable and silently relied upon. Now, as always, our discreet accomplices.

Frying Pan

In other houses, I always notice the kitchen. It may not necessarily be the handsomest room, or the most agreeable, but it is always the most interesting, the room where the essential takes place. In other rooms, you chatter, you slump, you watch TV, you read, you wash, you sleep, you make love, you put things away, you eat, all of which are activities in other respects essential too. But in the kitchen you operate, you transmute. It is there that innumerable metamorphoses are accomplished: cooking, emulsifying, infusing, blending of juices, of flavours, of colours, of textures. Quick preparations, barely sealed over a high flame, or things cooked over a slow simmer. Even when it is compact and scaled down, or frankly tiny, the kitchen has something of the magic cavern. It remains a place of secrets, of acts of dexterity and intuition; the place where one guesses and experiments, where foods pass from a raw to a cooked state, from a state of nature to the human sphere.

Today I have very little time for cooking. Too much work before the holidays, too many questions to resolve quickly before the general dispersal takes place. Just an omelette on the side. Eggs, herbs, a zest of cheese, a turn of the pepper mill, a trickle of olive oil. The frying pan, all-important, heavy, as it has to be, thick, black, not too large.

I am ignorant as to its history. Who invented the frying pan? Its existence is surely very ancient, probably going back into the mists of time. At this moment only the magnificent ingenuity of the object itself concerns me. It serves to separate the food from the fire, and to conduct the heat. It seems to me to unite in itself something of the bowl (a receptacle, preventing dispersion), something of the table (a flat surface above the flame, a parallel floor) and also something of the sandal (an interface, an intermediary, a frontier-thing). It is unique, however, in that it conducts heat, spreads and distributes it evenly: the omelette cooks around the edges as well as at the centre.

Do you know of any other thing that simultaneously separates and distributes? That protects from the fire and yet conducts it? Capable of collecting and holding, but also of transforming? It may be that our human skin acts as a kind of frying pan in respect of the world out there. A somewhat obscure hypothesis.

Razor

bathroom, summer morning

Only a few days left before the holidays. Always a curious moment: there is more to do than usual, many tasks to finish if I am to go away with any peace of mind. And yet I am already elsewhere, or nearly. At the same time occupied and preoccupied, disconnected. To get it all done, I have to get up unconscionably early. It is already light, but only just. For me, who am still on another planet in the mornings, this is a landscape from a distant galaxy. Rarefied atmosphere, excessive light. I take refuge in the bathroom, cover my face in shaving foam, hoping no doubt to be reintegrated into the solar system at least.

The razor is at the ready. That at least is reassuring. I am more than a little grateful to it for being there. It is a universal property of things, I know, that they stay in the same place. It would not be strictly accurate to say that they wait. But they do stay put. There they are, in their places, always on call. I feel a decidedly strong impulse of fellow feeling towards this razor. I have just arrived from I know not where, am not fully present as yet, have left myself rather in the lurch, and the world is incomplete, lacking most things (consistence, existence); I ask myself when and how my sense of reality is going to return – flat, regular, normal – and here is the razor, eminently normal, nickel, punctual, in the same place as before, same appearance. No change there. Small but steadfast.

I pass it under the warm water. As I shave, I start to wake up, slowly but surely. And with this new model, practically no chance of cutting myself. The skin is merely brushed lightly and the bristles are obliterated, give way to smoothness, to softness. I have a sudden image of the scythe, the fearfulness of the scythe, the terror of blades, the menace of knives. But the razor's edge is fairly tame. Protected, under control. The razor cuts without making an incision. It glides over the surface. My gratitude for this thing is growing all the time, so sure-footed, so safe. So entirely indispensable. How would you shave without a razor? You would have to wait until a beard grew, and then have the willpower to pluck it out, tuft by tuft, like the Jain in India, who pull out the hair of monks entering their community. I have no idea whether what works with hair would work with beards. Whatever the case, it would be extremely painful, and doubtless bloody. My gratitude for the razor reaches new heights.

While I rinse out the blade, the filings of stubble caught up in the shaving foam are left scattered around the sink. Bits of me, or are they already things? Whoever tries to ponder the relations between ourselves and things would do well to attend to this perpetual turning-to-matter, this thingifying of our bodies. Bits of bristle, tiny pieces of skin, ends of hair, fragments of nail, all constantly working their way loose from us. As if the edges of the body were ceaselessly and imperceptibly crossing over into the world of things.

Book

at home, summer Sunday

I am taking advantage of the new shelves to tidy and arrange my books. I do this at regular intervals, especially just before going on holiday. These strange objects, books, need to be put in order so as to free up one's head. To live among books breeds oddities of behaviour. The book-thing is so little like other things that you never know what to expect of it. On the one hand, it is only paper, boards and glue, a thing like all the other things of fixed mass – that get old, get dropped, get torn, get dirty and on occasion get burnt. On the other hand, this particular thing is also a voice, a face, a history, an idea, a memorial, an offensive, a struggle, an earthly existence, a folly, a stroke of genius, a mine of information, a recollection. Each book has its separate identity, its turn of the head, its gait. I can never think of them other than as persons. Fairly odd persons – dry, abrasive, inky, paginated, in appearance impassive – but persons nonetheless, endlessly capable of words and actions, hatching obscure plots or living out their passions in slow motion and with matchless intensity. These thing-persons maintain very close ties with my body, if difficult to describe. They are in some sense extensions of the body, like non-sentient limbs that are nevertheless lodged in one's physical memory, and part of the very fabric of one's sensibility.

For example: I know the precise location of nearly all of my books, even after an interval of years, despite successive removals and endless reorganising. I can recall too, with a few exceptions, all the books I have ever managed to rid myself of in the course of time, whose number is legion, lorry-loads of them. Of these vanished libraries I retain a shadowy impression, similar perhaps to the 'phantom limbs' of amputees. I make no clear distinction, basically, between the rows of shelves where all these visages are aligned, and what it is convenient to refer to as 'me'. This 'me' includes, up to a point, these perpendicular gatherings of pages, each with its silhouette, its profile, its past. No matter that there were, over the course of time, thousand upon thousand of similar ones, that many have gone, and that too many remain . . . That too is me.

Which is why, when I sort through the accumulated piles, the heaped titles, all mixed up in the course of work, I always have the sensation of putting things away in my head. I am making interior order, undoing knots and tangles. When the volumes clamber over each other and range themselves in no particular order, which is generally the case, I have the sensation that my mind is also a shadowy chaos, which is also generally the case.

Something that always intrigues me is how books manage to coexist peacefully with each other, side by side. On one level, this is of course normal and to be expected: nothing but paper, glue and boards, no risk of a revolution there. However, on the analogy of books as persons with histories, it is anything but comprehensible. I am always astonished that battles of the books are never reported. It so often happens that sworn enemies find themselves side by side on a shelf, pressed into an embrace. You would expect to come down one morning and find the shelves devastated, volumes creased and crumpled, one or other of them perhaps torn to bits, all over the floor. And yet nothing of the kind. Nothing, never. Try and work that one out if you can . . .

Compact Disc

at home, just before leaving

Time to pack my bags. Just before going away for the summer, I decide which music I am going to take with me. Like everyone – or in any case like an awful lot of you, everywhere. With the accompanying and very basic reflection that this activity was inconceivable to anyone at all only a few generations ago. Music back then was something that was played live, on an instrument, at street corners or in squares, in churches, in drawing rooms. It could not be captured and carried under the arm, or thrown into a bag. Except for those few people who could read a score, which was in any case music for reading, music without the sounds. Next there came, in succession, gramophones and needles, wax cylinders, shellac, magnetic tape, vinyl, cassettes. And then this thing, quasi-celestial, iridescent, occult yet familiar, which is the optical disc or compact disc: a wafer-thin silver orb, dazzling, translucent, unalterable. This thing of outrageous beauty – chaste, inaccessible – contains entire hours of music. Without variation. Without wear, at least in principle. Without distortion. A thing that lives an untroubled existence, that operates with light itself, like the prism and the rainbow, in a manner that is strangely troubling. An impervious thing which evokes the music of the spheres, the perfect world of the stars.

The disc, a form at once entirely new and archaic. The solar disc of the Egyptians. Ra in a fine plastic wafer, enclosing within itself all possible sounds, all encoded, compressed, covered with a fine translucent film. This thing of technology is also a thing of mystery. Educational articles have patiently explained to me a hundred times, in magazines and newspapers, what is involved. Encodings, digitising of signals. All of which I forget, because it does not interest me. Magical and incomprehensible are when the fine wafer, rigid and circular, is swallowed by the machine, and music fills the room with woodwind or voices, jazz or chamber music.

But this is already an old and out-of-date miracle, almost a relic, almost laughable. Many more feats of inclusion are to be expected from this charmed circle with the celestial reflections. Not just sounds. Images too: photos, paintings, entire museums. And moving images, videos, broadcasts, the archives of the world. Texts of all kinds, books, encyclopaedias, maps and charts, entire libraries, in all the languages, living and dead. This thing of iridescent plastic is well on its way to becoming the universal absorbent, which electronically captures all sounds and images and texts – the entire surging, innumerable, chaotic totality of music and film, literature and painting and photography.

I can see the day coming when everything has been captured on disc. Absolutely everything, from the Big Bang to the furthest galaxies, the entire universe digitalised, compacted, recorded, reduced to a single, easily transportable featherweight disc. And then we really can go on holiday. But *who* exactly will be doing the holidaying?

Fly Swatter

Mediterranean,
a summer evening

It rests on the edge of the sink, in the kitchen of this house overhanging the sea where I am spending some time. Immersed in a blue such as exists, to my knowledge, only in the middle of the Mediterranean. It is lying flat, a small rectangle of yellow plastic, cell-structured, at the end of a long, flexible handle. It is a fly swatter, a modern copy of an object from time past, from a time before insecticides, aerosols, diffusers, or those bluish lights that grill insects to death all night long; before modern times with their chemical mastery of the world.

This archaic leftover of a thing is devoid, utterly, of the slightest practical efficacy. Virtually impossible to kill a fly by this means. All right, one in every thousand. Looking at it, at first I did not even grasp what it was for, so precisely does it seem to serve no purpose at all. This is all the more peculiar in that very old things are usually so patently and unmistakably adapted to their function.

We must consider the conundrum from a different angle. The fly swatter is in fact intended to be useless, at least as far as the destruction of flies is concerned. It is not intended to kill flies. Instead it embodies a gesture of protest, of refusal. Of irritation. It says that this should not be, that this buzzing and droning is pointless. That these creatures are objectionable, insalubrious and stupid. That one must refuse them any quarter, shoo them away. That there can be no dialogue with flies. The swatter gesticulates so that they will go away. It yells at them that there will be no mercy, that they will all end up squashed, flattened, obliterated, without exceptions. Clearly, it has no intention of putting an end to a single one of them. But it flaps and creates a wind, so that they will remove themselves for ever. Which no doubt occasionally happens.

The fly swatter is not a utilitarian object, at least not primarily so. It is pure gesture, nothing more. Lying there on the sink, it is without meaning, it is at the outer limit of the absurd. It only becomes a fly swatter when it is held in the hand and waved about, when it is used to deal sharply and windily with the inopportune insects that have in the meantime already traded places. It merely drives away, without ever catching or killing; and with a view to achieving a measure of untroubled calm.

As such, it is an eminently philosophical thing. Philosophy likewise is without direct utility, without outcome, in the first instance; it is pure gesture, existing only when taken in hand and set in movement; dedicated to getting rid of bother and achieving a state of calm. It has perhaps too seldom been remarked that the philosophical gesture is characterised by the questions it avoids rather than by those it asks. A large part of the method of a philosopher, for me at least, consists in chasing questions away, putting them to flight, making them scatter by administering sharp blows. Let us stop thinking of philosophers as caught up in all the noise and blather of intellectual history. In fact, philosophers refuse flatly to engage with questions that strike them as empty, importunate or repugnant.

The question swatter of the philosopher delivers sharp blows. To abandon a problem, or an entire conception of the world, without a word, without any justification, without abiding the trick questions, refusing even to lend them an ear. To make oneself deaf, enduringly, to whatever is without interest; to advance without caring if we falter, obstinate, almost obtuse – might that not also be a model of thinking?

Over To You?

One has to know when to stop an experiment. This one could go on indefinitely, and this journal of things could be without end. I am stopping here, because infinite stories must necessarily be interrupted. Up to you to continue, with your own things, different no doubt from mine, or else differently pursued. All the more so, in that there is always something inconclusive, and impossible to unravel, in the very idea of the thing. Up to you to discover in turn what is revealed by that simple question: 'So, how are things?' It remains open.

For my part, I have by now the rudiments of a reply. How are things going? Well, they go to the beach, they go to school, they stay at home; they are doing wonderfully, they are going to the dogs, they are going with the stream, and against the current, they come and they go, their end is as their beginning, they are doing their thing where you are, and they are doing their thing where you are not. That is what I would say on the subject.

If you think these are idiocies, that I am merely playing with words, you would not be wrong, although I have a reason for doing so: for I have learnt over the past year that there is no other means of telling how things are, than by sparking off brief flares on the anvil of words inside one's head; or like ricochets off the surface of water.

Let me add that things do neither well nor ill: they are never ill, nor well; that, even broken or discarded, they are as they are, guileless and absurd.

I would add that things are frequently the bearers of our thoughts, releasing them, accompanying them, even diverting them from their course. There is little chance, at this moment, of your thinking independently about beavers, or the court dress of the Samurai, or the ceremonial clothes of the Eskimos, or Prussian armour, or Palaeolithic burial mounds, or anything else of this nature. Except as the result of an encounter, in a museum or a flea market, of this or that object which evinces one or other of these separate realities. There are whole populations of ideas that are only ours courtesy of things and our chance encounters with them. A dependency at once casual and profound.

Finally, I would say that our attitude to things is an index of our relationship to ourselves. If they fascinate and hold us in thrall, we no longer know who we are. But if we repulse and scorn them, we fall equally wide of ourselves. It is between these two poles that we should steer a course, always ready for the encounter with things, noting how they mingle or meddle with us, how they encroach upon our supposed freedoms. We are not 'centred' upon ourselves until we can bear to admit that such a centre does not exist.

You want to know how things are? Very simple: they are as you are yourself. Reciprocally so. Each and every thing is the measure of man. Up to you to be neither too rigid nor too wayward. Up to you to treat things as you treat your self.

Apropos of which, and in case I forget: this morning I happened to run across the man who asked the question. I still don't know who he is. As I went towards him he held out his hand and said, 'Well! So how are you? . . .'